A BEGINNER'S GUIDE TO MAKING
ELECTRONIC GADGETS

2ND EDITION

BY R.H. WARRING

TAB BOOKS Inc.
BLUE RIDGE SUMMIT, PA 17214

Books by the Author

No. 1142 *84 Practical IC Projects You Can Build*
No. 1493 *Electronic Components Handbook for Circuit Designers*
No. 1553 *Understanding Electronics-2nd Edition*
No. 1593 *Understanding Digital Electronics*
No. 1673 *Robots and Robotology*
No. 1853 *Logic Made Easy*

SECOND EDITION

SECOND PRINTING

Printed in the United States of America

Reproduction or publication of the content in any manner, without express permission of the publisher, is prohibited. No liability is assumed with respect to the use of the information herein.

Library of Congress Cataloging in Publication Data

Warring, R. H. (Ronald Horace), 1920-
    A beginner's guide to making electronic gadgets.

    Includes index.
    1. Electronics—Amateurs' manuals.   I. Title.
TK9965.W38   1984   621.381   84-16438
ISBN 0-8306-0793-5
ISBN 0-8306-1793-0 (pbk.)

Contents

Introduction

This is intended as a mainly practical book on interesting—and useful—electronic circuits that are simple to construct and get working. Most of these working circuits—and there are some hundred described in all—are based on semiconductor devices (mostly transistors) and standard miniature components, all of which should be readily obtainable from shops or mail order houses specializing in the supply of amateur radio or electronic experimenter components.

The manner in which many of the circuits work, and can be modified, is explained in practical terms so the reader can acquire a sound background knowledge of practical electronics as he progresses through the book.

No previous knowledge of electronics—or even of electronic components—is needed to get started, for essential basic information on this particular subject is given in the first three chapters. It is assumed, however, that the builder of these circuits can use an electric soldering iron and has some familiarity with laying out and wiring up physical circuits.

The chapters on Coupling, Amplifiers, Oscillators, and Outputs have been included to broaden further the reader's background knowledge of practical electronics, again with many working circuits illustrating the principles involved. These represent the building blocks on which many more complicated circuits are constructed.

The remainder of the book is devoted to descriptions of individual circuits which come under the general category of electronic gadgets. A number of these have been inspired by, or are based on, original circuit designs which have been published elsewhere, i.e., the author has experimented with these circuits and adapted them or variations for this book.

A number of circuits are also based on original Mullard designs—circuits which have become virtually standard electronic practice and widely used both by amateur and professional constructors. True originality in simple electronic circuitry is now comparatively rare—the basic factors of such circuits being established by the characteristics of semiconductor devices themselves.

In this new second edition, material has been added concerning the newer types of integrated circuits. In addition, you will find that the sections about component specifications has been increased. Lastly, I would like to encourage you to experiment with these circuit designs so that you may use them for your own specific purposes.

Chapter 1

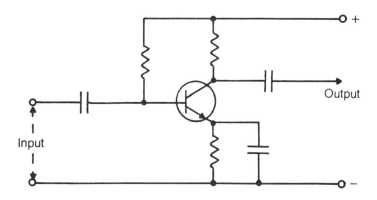

Transistors

Let's begin by learning what transistors are and what they can do. (Readers who already know how transistors work and how to connect them can skip this chapter, but they may still find it useful for reference from time to time.)

Transistor is the name given to a whole variety of semiconductor or solid-state electronic components (usually called devices), with characteristics more like the old-fashioned triode radio tubes than similar electronic components like resistors and capacitors. While transistors form the *working* part of electronic circuits, resistors and capacitors usually adjust working *levels* in a particular circuit. This is rather like the transistor being an *engine*, and the resistors and capacitors in the circuit the *control* for the engine.

Common types of transistors are distinguished by having three terminals connected to the semiconductor material from which they are made. This distinguishes them from a *diode*, which is another semiconductor device with two terminals, and more complex semiconductor circuits or ICs (integrated ciruits). However, some transistors apparently have only two terminals. In such cases, the third is inside connecting to a metallic case. The type used in simple circuits, with three terminals (usually thin wires), show these emerging from the bottom of the transistor case. Inside they connect to internal parts of the transistor known as the *emitter, base,*

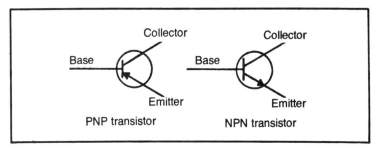

Fig. 1-1. Symbols and terminal connections of PNP and NPN transistors.

and *collector* shown in symbolic form in Fig. 1-1. This forms the picture of a transistor used in circuit diagrams.

It will be noticed that two different types of transistors are shown—a PNP type and a NPN type. This is really a difference in the *polarity* of the transistor and indicates the way it has to be connected in a circuit. The arrow on the emitter (in the transistor symbol) points from a positive to a negative polarity in a circuit where the transistor is normally conducting.

The basic rules to remember when connecting a transistor to a circuit or designing a transistor circuit are:

1. The base must be one terminal of the *input* circuit.
2. The collector must be one terminal of the *output* circuit.
3. With a PNP transistor, the polarity must always be such that the *collector* is Negative relative to the connection to the emitter.
4. With an NPN transistor the polarity of connection must always be such that the *collector* is positive relative to the connection to the emitter.

It is important to get these connections right, for if a transistor is connected the wrong way in a circuit it can be "blown" and permanently damaged.

What can be a little confusing at first is the variety of shapes and sizes of transistor bodies, plus the fact that the three terminal wires do not always emerge from the bottom of the body, or case, in the same way. Some common arrangements are shown in Fig. 1-2. These cover nearly all transistor types most likely to be used in simple circuits except power transistors.

If the three wire leads emerge *in line*, these may be evenly spaced (usually from a circular shape), or unevenly spaced (usually from a rectangular shape). If they are *evenly* spaced then there will

2

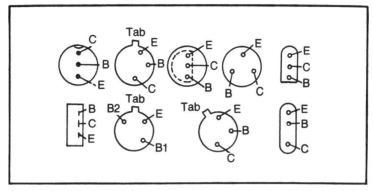

Fig. 1-2. Common arrangements of transistor leads: E = emitter, B = base, C = collector.

be a colored or white dot marked on the side of the transistor opposite one of the end leads. This identifies that lead as the *collector*. The center lead is the *base* and the other end lead the *emitter*.

With uneven spacing the end lead most widely spaced is the *collector*. The center lead is the *base* again and the other end lead the *emitter*.

The other alternative is a triangular arrangement of the leads usually found on a circular shaped transistor body with a flange on the bottom. Here two leads will be opposite one another in line with the center. The third will be at the apex of the triangle. This third wire is the *base*. Viewing the transistor from the bottom, the right-hand lead is then the *collector* and the left-hand lead the *emitter*.

The common form of *power transistor* is larger than other transistors and commonly has the shape shown in Fig. 1-3. This shape has been standardized by most manufacturers. As mentioned previously, power transistors usually have only two external leads; they are in the form of metal pins. These emerge from the case with

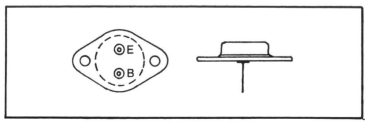

Fig. 1-3. Typical form of a power transistor. The collector is connected internally to the case.

markings to identify them as *emitter* (e) and *base* (b). The collector is usually internally connected to the metal case. Thus, to complete connection in a circuit, the third connection has to be made to the case in some suitable way (e.g., to one of the screws used to mount the transistor in position).

Transistor specifications in manufacturers' or suppliers' catalogues normally state the outline as a TO number; common Transistor Outlines and their numbers are shown in Fig. 1-4. By knowing the TO number you can, from these diagrams, determine both the physical size of transistor specified and the lead configuration. It's a useful reference.

To complete our general picture of transistors, all are made from either germanium or silicon semiconductor material. These are known as germanium transistors or silicon transistors. Germanium transistors are generally cheaper, but this type of material is more readily damaged by heat. Thus germanium transistors cannot be used at working temperatures in excess of 100° C. Silicon transistors can be operated at working temperatures of 150° C. or more, if necessary, without damage.

There are electrical differences, too. Germanium transistors have lower voltage losses, but higher leakage currents. Silicon

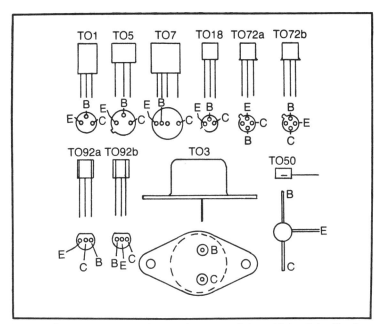

Fig. 1-4. Common transistor shapes, shown actual size, with lead identification.

4

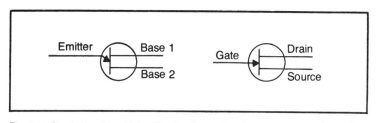

Fig. 1-5. Symbol and lead identification for unijunction transistor (left) and field effect transistor (right). Both types can be PNP (arrowhead inwards) or NPN (arrowhead outwards).

transistors have very much lower leakage currents, can accommodate higher voltages without damage, and are particularly advantageous where higher output powers are required.

Silicon transistors are usually made by the planar process and are often referred to as *silicon planar transistors*. Germanium transistors are made by either the alloy-junction or alloy-diffusion process. All three are basically junction type transistors where the construction produces definite junctions between the base, emitter, and collector elements. Today, the advantages of silicon transistors have long since made them the most popular type.

Field-effect transistor or FETs, are a later development, and here the construction is quite different. It may still end up looking like an ordinary transistor, but its electronic characteristics are quite different. Its elements are known as the *source, gate* and *drain* (equivalent only vaguely to the emitter, base and collector, respectively, of a conventional transistor) and it is given a different symbol as shown in Fig. 1-5.

Another type of semiconductor is the *unijunction* transistor; the description applies specifically to the type of construction. Effectively, it has one emitter and two base terminals. Field effect transistors, however, may be either the junction type or insulated-gate construction.

BASIC CIRCUITS

The three basic ways in which a transistor is connected between an input and an output are shown in Fig. 1-6. These are known as circuit configurations.

To function, a transistor also has to be provided with bias, which is really a voltage applied to, or current flow between, the emitter and base. This bias determines the working characteristics of the transistor.

The common-emitter circuit configuration is most widely fa-

5

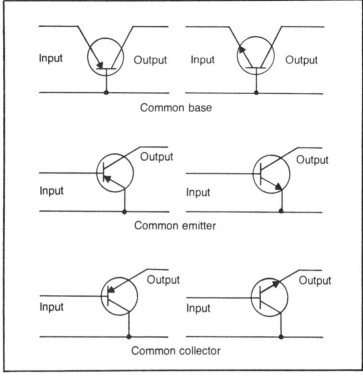

Fig. 1-6. Basic transistor circuit configuration. PNP transistors left; NPN transistors right.

vored for transistors since a single battery will supply the bias in the emitter circuit and also the power in the output or collector circuit.

TRANSISTOR TEST CIRCUIT

The circuit shown in Fig. 1-7 is an example of *current* bias, and can be used to test the performance of individual low power junction transistors. Although simple, this is actually quite a clever bias circuit for it provides automatic dc compensation for transistor variations. The current flowing is determined by the value of R1 and the battery voltage. Any increase in collector current will lower the voltage at the collector because of the increased voltage drop across R2. This will reduce the bias to automatically adjust the collector current to a lower level.

This circuit can be built on a simple board as shown in Fig. 1-8. Transistor connections are made not to the transistor, but to a transistor socket; this enables different transistors to be plugged in

6

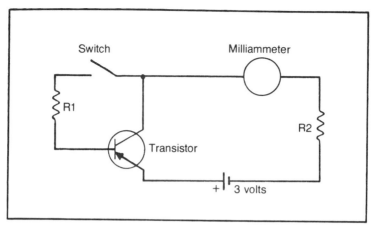

Fig. 1-7. Simple current bias circuit which can be used for testing transistors R1 = 60,000 ohms, R2 = 1000 ohms.

for testing and easy removal. The ammeter shown has a 0.25 or 0.5 milliamp range. Resistor values are: R1 = 60 K (60,000 ohms) and R2 = 100 K (100,000 ohms). A switch (preferably a push-button) is connected on the emitter circuit. A 3-volt battery connects to the + and − terminals for testing PNP transistors. For testing NPN transistors *the battery connections must be made the other way* (battery + to circuit − and battery − to circuit +).

Plugging a transistor into the holder should immediately give a reading on the milliammeter. This will be the *leakage current* of the transistor. Closing the switch should then give a higher current reading, indicating that the transistor is working. A faulty transistor will indicate the following:

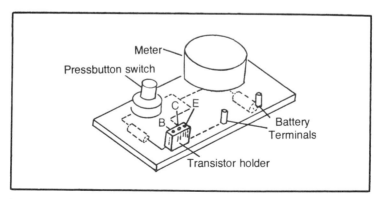

Fig. 1-8. Component layout for transistor tester. Resistors and wiring connections completed under panel.

1. Open circuit transistors—no reading when plugged in and no reading when switch is depressed.
2. Isolated transistors—high reading when plugged in.

The component values for this circuit have been chosen so that the current gain of the transistor can also be measured; this is expressed as h_{le} on transistor specifications. Simply make a note of the actual reading in milliamps when switch is depressed and multiply by 20. This will be the h_{le} figure for that transistor.

Since leakage currents are generally minute—especially with silicon transistors—and small differences in meter needle position are difficult to read, it would be better to use an 0 to 100 microammeter in the circuit for leakage current measurement. The performance of individual transistors of the same or similar type can then be compared, and the best transistor can be selected for a particular circuit. Remember to replace the microammeter with the milliammeter for measuring gain as the current with the switch depressed will be much higher than the microammeter can safely take.

To make the test circuit goof proof, terminate the wires connecting to the meter in a 2-pin socket. Microammeter and milliammeter are then each wired to a 2-pin plug. This makes it easier to change from one meter to the other.

Chapter 2

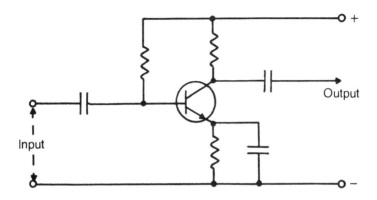

Equivalent Transistors

Transistors of specific type number, produced by individual manufacturers, have individual characteristics, although these may vary even within one type. Circuits commonly specify a particular type of transistor or equivalent. This is really a matter of availability. A particular transistor type specified may not be obtainable when wanted, so an equivalent must be used to work with the other components and component values given in the original circuit design. The circuit could also work with quite a different type of transistor, but this would normally mean altering most, or all, the component values.

Transistors of one make may not have an exact equivalent in another make, so quoted equivalents are normally near-equivalents, implying that they should work with the same circuit component values. Since literally thousands of different types of transistors have been produced, a list of equivalents could (and does) fill a whole book. In fact, there are reference books devoted exclusively to listing transistor equivalents; the serious electronic experimenter will find it useful to add one to his library. TAB book 1470 is one such reference. Book 1471 is another.

As a general guide, the following section lists common transistor types according to usual application. The list is restricted to transistor types readily available in the U.S. and Great Britain and is by no means complete. But by keeping the listings short, and confining them to good quality transistors, there is less possibility of confusion in deciding on an equivalent type. Basically, all transistors in the same group can be regarded as equivalents when functioning in the *same type of circuits*. It does not follow that their performance will be the same in such circuits, however, nor that the same circuit component values can be used. Suitable equivalents are therefore also given, where practicable. Equivalents listed should be a satisfactory direct substitute in the same circuit. Coding given in brackets designates the transistor package style.

Germanium PNP—low power general duty:

TYPE	EQUIVALENT(S)
OC41 (TO1)	CV7042, ASY56, ASY57, OC72, 2N65, 2N104, 2N109, 2N111, 2N112, 2N113, 2N114, 2N123.
OC42 (TO1)	CV8252, ASY57, ASY58, OC72, 2N65, 2N104, 2N109, 2N111, 2N112, 2N114.
OC72 (TO1)	CV5713, CV7006, CV8440, OC308, OC604, NKT 121, 2N281, 2N1305, 2SB89, AC128, AC131, AC132, AC151, AC153, ACY36.
OC75 (TO1)	CV5439, OC304, OC604, NKT213, 2N41, 2N1303, 2SB77, 2SB89, AC122, AC125, AC126, AC131
	AC151, AC163, ACY30, ASY58, ASY59.
OC81 (TO1)	NKT271, 2N1305, AC128.
OC81D (TO1)	AC128.
AC128 (TO1)	CV9779, OC74, OC318, NKT281, 2N467, 2SB222, 2SB415, AC117, AC124, AC153, GET110.

**Germanium PNP—radio
frequency amplifiers and oscillators:**

TYPE	EQUIVALENT(S)
2N3325 (TO18)	
NKT603F (TO7)	

10

NKT613F (TO7)
NKT674F (TO7)

OC44 (TO1)	CV5710, CV7003, OC170, OC171, OC410, OC613, 2N1303, 2SA15, AF101, AF117, AF126, ASY55.
OC45 (TO1)	CV5105, CV7004, OC390, OC612, 2N218, 2N1303, 2SA12, 2SA49, AF101, AF116, AF126, AF127, ASY54.
AF118 (TO7)	CV10276, 2SA76, 2N327, 2N328, 2N329, 2N935, 2N936, 2N945, 2N1035, 2N1232.
AF139 (TO72a)	AF148, AF239, 2N502, 2N700, 2N1158, 2N1727, 2N1728, 2N1790, 2N2363, 2SA54, 2SA256, 2SA257.

AF200U (TO72b)
AF239 (TO72a)
AF279 (TO50)

Germanium PNP—low power audio frequency amplifiers:

TYPE	EQUIVALENT(S)
NKT214 (TO1)	2N1305, AC115, AC128, ASY63, ACY34, ACY35.
NKT217 (TO1)	ASY13, ASY51, ASY52.
NKT274 (TO1)	2N1303, AC128.
NKT211 (TO1)	ACY18, AC128, ASY82, ASY84.
NKT212 (TO1)	2N1305, AC127, AC128, AC131, AC132, AC166, AC167, AC177, ACY36.
NKT213(TO1)	2N1309, ACY23, ACY31, AC122, AC128, AC138, AC156, AC165.
AC126 (TO1)	OC71, OC81, OC303, OC304, KNT219, 2N506, 2SB219, 2SB415, AC122, AC151, AC163.
AC107 (TO1)	CV7008, OC303, OC304, 2N1305, NKT216, AC117, AC122, AC128, AC151, ACY32, 2SB178.

TYPE	EQUIVALENT(S)
AC128 (TO1)	CV9779, OC74, OC318, NKT281, 2N467, 2SB222,
	2SB415, AC117, AC124, AC153, GET110.
OC71 (TO1)	KNT214, 2N280, 2N1305, 2SB77, AC122, AC125,
	AC151, AC163, ACY35.

Germanium PNP—medium power
AF amplifiers, medium current suitability:

TYPE	EQUIVALENT(S)
ACY17 (TO5)	CV7376, CV9482, NKT237, 2SB218.
ACY18 (TO5)	CV7436, CV8130, KNT238.
ACT19 (TO5)	CV7436, CV10183, NKT239.
ACY20 (TO5)	CV7438, CV9483, KNT240, 2N524, 2N525, 2N526,
	2N527, 2N597.
ACY21 (TO5)	CV7439, CV8259, NKT241, 2N524, 2N525, 2N597,
	2N650.
ACY22 (TO5)	CV10550, NKT242, ACY33, 2N315, 2N317, 2N598,
	2N1204, 2N1384, 2N1478, 2N1495.
ACY39 (TO5)	NKT244.
ACY41 (TO5)	NKT245.
ACT44 (TO5)	
2N1303 (TO5)	CV7352, NKT135, ASY26, ASY57, ASY63, ASY64,
	2N1997, 2N1998.
2N1305 (TO5)	CV353, CV9536, ASY54, ASY58, ASY63, NKT135,
	2N466, 2N1309, 2N1997, 2N1998.
2N1307 (TO5)	CV7354, NKT137, ACY29, ACY30, ASY27, ASY55,
	ASY59, ASY63, 2N1309, 2N1997, 2N1998.
2N1309 (TO5)	CV7355, CV9481, ASY59, ASY60, ASY63, 2N1997,
	2N1998.
ASY26(TO5)	CV9730, OC390, NKT135, 2N799, 2SA155,
	ASY24,
	ASY48, ASY56, ASY64, ACY20, BSY24.
ASY27 (TO5)	CV10275, OC304, NKT135, 2N36, 2SB101, AC163,

OC83 (TO1)	ASY30, ASY48, ASY54, ASY57, ASY66. CV8724, CV9259, NKT223, AC128, AC152, ACY30, ASY58, ASY59.
OC84 (TO1)	CV5416, NKT211, AC128, ASY59.
AC118K (XO)	
AC151 (TO1)	OC303, OC304, NKT216, 2N238, 2SB101, 2SB415, AC122, AC125.
AC151R (TO1)	
AC152(TO1)	OC303, OC304, KNT281, 2N238, 2SB101, 2SB415 AC117, AC124, AC125, AC132, ASY48, GET110.
AC153	OC318, NKT281, 2N467, 2SB222, 2SB415, AC117, AC124, AC128, GET110.

Germanium NPN/AF
amplifiers, medium current suitability:

TYPE	EQUIVALENT(S)
2N1302 (TO5)	NKT34, 2N634, 2N635, 2N636, 2N1304, 2N1306 2N1308, 2N1891, 2N1993, 2N1994, 2N1995.
2N1304 (TO5)	CV7349, CV9261, NKT734, 2N634, 2N635, 2N636, 2N1302, 2N1306, 2N1891, 2N1993, 2N1994, 2N1995.
2N1306 (TO5)	CV7350, CB10686, NKT736, 2N634, 2N635, 2N636, 2N1891, 2N1993, 2N1994, 2N1995.
2N1308 (TO5)	2N1302, 2N1304, 2N1306, 2N1891, 2N1993, 2N1994, 2N1995.
ASY28 (TO5)	
ASY29 (TO5)	CV9040, OC400, NKT734, 2N211, 2SA255, AF101.
NKT713	ASY86, ASY88, AC127, AC128, AC132, AC168, AC172, AC175.
NKT773	AC130, AC157.

AC127 (TO1)	CV9778, NKT713, 2SD100, 2SD104, 2SD105, 2N59
	2N60, 2N61, 2N402, 2N403, 2N611, 2N726,
	2N1221,
	2N1280.
AC176 (TO1)	CV10675, NKT781
AC176K (X9a)	
AC187K (X9a)	

Germanium PNP—high power

TYPE	EQUIVALENT(S)
OC19 (TO3)	AD140. AD149.
OC25 (TO3)	CV7085, CV8982, AD149, OC28, 2N297, 2N418,
	2N420, 2N443, 2N458, 2N463.
OC28 (TO3)	CB7085, CV8342, NKT401, 2N456, 2S42, 2SB424,
	AD148, ASZ15, AUY22.
OC29 (TO3)	CV7083, CV8356, NKT402, 2N457, 2N457, 2SB86, 2SB425,
	AD150, ESZ16, AUY21, OC28, OC35.
OC35 (TO3)	CV7084, CV9264, NKT404, 2N352, 2SB86, 2SB425,
	ASZ17, AUY21, OC28, OC29, OC36.
OC36 (TO3)	CV7086, CV8480, NKT403, 2N157,
	2N1666, 3N1668, 2N2526, 2SB87, 2SB424,
	AD132, ASY18, ASZ18, AUY22, OC28,
	OC29, OC35.
NKT403 (TO3)	AD105, AU103, AUY32, ADY23, ADY24, ASZ18,
	2N458, 2N574, 2N677, 2N678, 2N1021, 2N1022,
	2N1029.
NKT404 (TO3)	AD104, AD131, AD140, AD152, ASZ16, ASZ17,
	AUY33, AU103, OC29, 2N443, 2N458, 2N574,
	22N677.
NKT405 (TO3)	AU103.
AL102 (TO3)	

AD133 (TO3)	2N1146, 2SB236, ADZ11, ADZ12.
AD136 (TO3)	2AD138, ADZ11, 2N278, 2N442, 2N443, 2N511, 2N512, 2N513.
AD140 (TO3)	NKT404, AD149.
AD142 (TO3)	OC26, OC27, 2N301A, AD133, ADZ12.
AD149 (TO3)	OC28, OC36, 2N456, 2S42, 2SB426, C138, AD148.
AD150 (TO3)	OC28, OC36, 2N456, 2S42, 2SB426, AC138, AD140, AD149.
AD161 (MD17c)	CV9777.
AD162 (MD17c)	CB9777, 2SB426.

Silicon NPN, general purpose, small signal:

TYPE	EQUIVALENT(S)
2N3708 (TO92a)	BC107.
2N3709 (TO92a)	BC107.
2N3710 (TO92a)	BC107.
2N3711 (TO92a)	
2N3904 (TO92b)	CV11041.
2N4124 (TO92b)	

Silicon NPN—radio frequency amplifiers and oscillators:

BF115 (TO72b)	CV10243.
BF167 (TO72b)	
BF173 (TO72b)	
BFY90 (TO72a)	CV10533.
BF194 (MM10b)	
BF195 (MM10b)	
BF254 (TO92za)	
BF255 (TO92za)	
2N3663 (TO98a)	BF173.
2N4292 (u29)	

Silicon NPN—audio frequency amplifiers:

TYPE	EQUIVALENT(S)
2N3707 (TO92a)	BC107.

Type	Equivalent(s)
N2930 (TO18)	CV7493, CV8467, CV10416, BC107, 2N243, 2N244, 2N560, 2N698.
2N2484 (TO18)	CV7738, CV9133, CV9368, 2N930, BCY66, BFY26.
2N2924 (TO98a)	CV11046, BC107.
2N2926 (TO98a)	BC107.
2N3391A (TO98a)	
2N4286 (u29)	BC107.
2N5088 (TO92b)	
BC109 (TO18)	CV10769, CV10806.
BC149 (MM10)	
BC169 (TO92a)	BC109.
BC184L (TO92a)	
BC269 (TO18)	
PN109 (RO97Aa)	
PN109 (RO97Aa)	
PN930 (RO97Aa)	

Silicon NPN—general purpose switching:

TYPE	EQUIVALENT(S)
BSX20 (TO18)	
BSX60 (TO5)	
BSX61 (TO5)	
P346A (TO18)	
2N706 (TO18)	CV9211, BXY20, BXY62, BXY70, 2N703, 2N708, 2N743, 2N744, 2N753, 2N756, 2N757, 2N1199.
2N2369A (TO18)	CV7555, CV9564.
2N3702 (TO92a)	CV10564.
2N3703 (TO92a)	CV10682.
2N4036 (TO5)	CV10548.
2N4291 (u29)	
BC126 (RO97)	
BCY30 (TO9)	CV7344, CV9430, BCY29.
BCY31 (TO5)	CV7344, CV8760, CV9247, BCY27, BCY28.
BC160 (TO5)	
BC303 (TO5)	
BFX29 (TO5)	
BFX87 (TO5)	

BFX88 (TO5)   CV10629.
40362 (TO5)
40406 (TO5)

Field Effect Transistors

TYPE   EQUIVALENT(S)
2N3819 (TO92c)   CV10684.
2N3823 (RO97Ab)   CV10832, CV11004.
2N4303 (RO97Ab)
2N5163 (RO97Ab)
2N5457 (RO97Ab)
2N5458 (RO97Ab)
2N5459 (RO97Ab)

Unijunction Transistors

TYPE   EQUIVALENT(S)
2N2646 (TO18)   CV9695.
T1543 (TO92e)
2N2160 (TO5)

Chapter 3

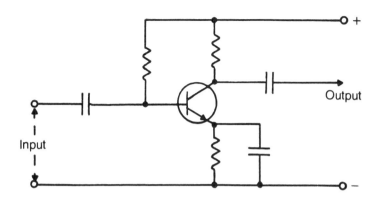

Other Circuit Components

Resistors used in transistor circuits are invariably of sub-miniature or miniature type, usually of carbon film construction. Such resistors have high stability and little self-generated noise, both characteristics are highly valued in transistor circuits. Typical shapes and sizes are shown in Fig. 3-1.

Resistance values normally follow a standard series: 1.0, 1.2, 1.5, 1.8, 2.2, 2.7, 3.3, 3.9, 4.7, 5.6, 6.8, and 8.2. There is a very good reason for this. Preferred values are based on a *logarithmic* scale, so that the next number up, or down, represents an approximately constant *percentage* change in resistance value.

Actual resistance values in ohms thus follow the series 10, 12, 15, 18, 22, etc. up to 1000. A value of 1000 ohms is usually described as 1 kilohm, written 1K. Values in kilohms then run 1, 1.2, 1.5, 1.8, 2.2, and so on up to 1000 kilohm, or 1 megohm, written 1 Meg. Values in megohms then follow in the same way—1.0, 1.2, 1.5, etc.

The physical size of a resistor is no indication of its resistance value. All values of similar make and type are usually the same size. The actual resistance value is marked by a color code consisting of four colored rings around the body of the resistor. See Fig. 3-2. These colors are read starting from the ring nearest to the end of the resistor.

The complete color code is:

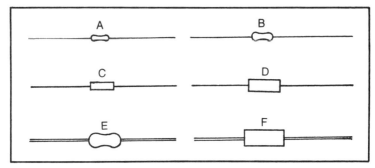

Fig. 3-1. Examples of sub-miniature and miniature resistors actual size. A, B, C & D are carbon film. E is metal oxide. F is carbon film.

Color	Value	Color	Value
black	0	green	5
brown	1	blue	6
red	2	violet	7
orange	3	grey	8
yellow	4	white	9

The number corresponding to the *first* color (first ring) gives the *first* digit of the value. The number corresponding to the second color (second ring) gives the second digit of the value. The number corresponding the the third color (third ring) gives the number of zeros to be added to the value.

For example: if the color is green, blue, orange—

First color: green = 5 = first digit
Second color: blue = 6 = second digit so we have 56
Third color: orange = 3 = number of zeros to be added

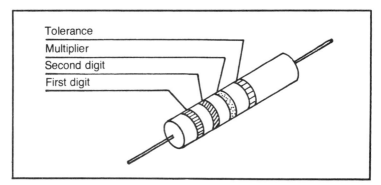

Fig. 3-2. Resistor color coding

Finally giving 56,000 ohms or 56 K ohms as the resistor's resistance value.

So far the fourth color band has been disregarded. This gives the tolerance of the resistor and so can be ignored for most purposes. The tolerance code is as follows:

brown ± 1 percent
red ± 2 percent
gold ± 5 percent
silver ± 10 percent

Thus, if the previous example—green, blue, orange—was followed by a silver band, this would indicate a 56 K ohm resistor with a tolerance of ± 10 percent.

The only other important thing about a resistor is its power rating. This is given in watts, e.g. 1/10 watt, 1/4 watt, 1/2 watt, 1 watt, etc. Again this is only significant in circuits when the wattage rating of the resistors used is at least as great as the value of circuit voltage multiplied by maximum current (in amps) flowing in that circuit. Average *electronic gadget* circuits use 1/2 watt resistors throughout. If not, there is a danger of the resistor becoming overheated and permanently damaged.

Variable resistors are generally known as potentiometers and have quite a different construction and physical appearance. The two main types used in simple circuits are carbon elements and "skeleton" types—see Fig. 3-3. Carbon potentiometers are adjustable by a knob fitted to the spindle. With a skeleton type potentiometer, adjustment of the setting is made by screwdriver adjustment in the central slot.

Fig. 3-3. Conventional potentiometer (left with carbon or wire-wound element. Skeleton potentiometers (right) are designed to connect directly into circuit panels or circuit boards.

Resistance values with potentiometers again usually follow the preferred series, but not so closely spaced, e.g., 1 K, 2.2 K, 4.7 K, 10 K, 22 K, 47 K, 100 K, etc. They are commonly referred to as nominal values in circuits, e.g., 1 K, 2 K, 5 K, 10 K, etc.

Capacitors are made in a wide range of sizes, shapes and materials. Ceramic capacitors are widely favored for transistor circuits because of their small size. They are usually *plate* shape for pF values from 22 to above 6800, and *disc* shape for values from 1000 pF up to 0.1 μF (i.e. 0.001 μF to 0.1 μF). Moulded mica types are also used for μF values. For large values, 0.1 μF up, electrolytic capacitors are normally used. These are larger and readily identified by their metallic casing (see Fig. 3-4). Electrolytic capacitors are *polarized*; this means they must be connected with the + end marked on the capacitor body to circuit positive.

Capacity values are usually marked on the capacitor body; a color code is also sometimes used. The color code used today is:

black = 1
brown = 10
red = 100
orange = 1000
yellow = 10000

Other colors can be usually ignored as these refer to tolerance and/or temperature characteristics.

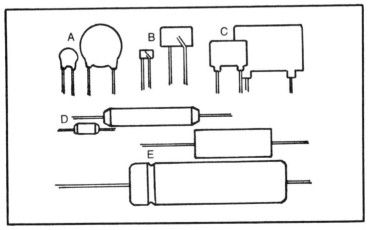

Fig. 3-4. Capacitor types and approximate range of physical sizes (shown actual size). A = ceramic disc. B = ceramic plate. C = silvered mica. D = polyester. E= electrolytic.

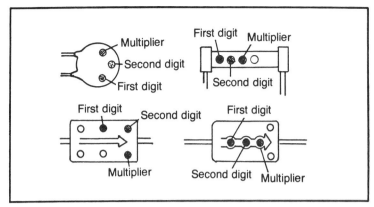

Fig. 3-5. Capacitor color codes.

The colors are then read similarly to the resistor color code, as:

$$\left.\begin{array}{l} \text{first digit} \\ \text{second digit} \\ \text{multiplier} \end{array}\right\} \quad \textit{see} \text{ Fig. 3-5.}$$

Miniature *variable capacitors* suitable for simple transistor circuits are usually plastic dielectric where the size is about 1 inch square by ½ inch thick (typical values up to 500 pF), with spindle and knob adjustment. Even smaller mica-dielectric trimmer capacitors may be used, adjustable by screwdriver. Typical capacity values extend to 500 pF. Miniature airspaced variable capacitors are also available, although maximum capacity is usually of the order of 150-200 pF. The latter type are often fitted with trimmer capacitance as standard.

Alternative types, where size is not important, are solid dielectric tuning capacitors (up to 500 pF), and larger air-spaced tuning capacitors, single, double and triple ganged. Values again usually extend up to 500 pF (Fig. 3-6).

Capacitors have a *voltage* rating rather than a power rating. This simply means that they are constructed to work at *any* circuit voltage up to the rated figure as a maximum. However the higher the voltage rating the larger the physical size of electrolytic capacitor (for a given capacitance value), so in the interest of compact circuitry, use electrolytic capacitors with a voltage rating matching the maximum voltage of the circuit.

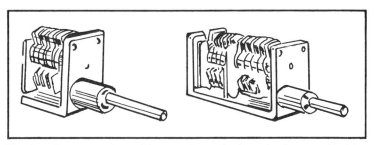

Fig. 3-6. Examples of variable capacitors, single and twin-gang. Variable capacitors sometimes have reduction gearing between the operating spindle and vane movement.

COMPONENT SYMBOLS

In circuit diagrams the following symbols are used:

> C for capacitors
> D for diodes
> L for coils (inductances)
> R for resistors
> RFC for radio frequency chokes

MICROFARADS AND PICOFARADS

Confusion can often arise when capacitor values are quoted in both microfarads (μF) and picofarads (pF) on the same circuit diagram, especially as sometimes the actual unit symbol is omitted. The basic rule in this case is to remember that a picofarad is one *millionth* of a microfarad:

$$1 \text{ pF} = \frac{\mu F}{1,000,000}$$

It therefore follows as a general rule that where *whole number* values are given for capacitors with no symbol following, then the value is specified in picofarads (pF). For example if 250 is marked against a capacitor then its value is probably 250 pF. This, of course, is the same as 0.00025 μF.

Capacitor values in microfarads (μF) are generally—but not invariably—decimal fractions e.g., 0.01, 0.005, etc. So if a decimal fraction value appears without a symbol this will certainly be microfarads.

For example, if 0.02 is quoted against a capacitor, then its most likely value is 0.02 μF.

24

The exception is that whole number values of capacitance in microfarads can also be quoted. Electrolytic capacitor values may even range up to 10,000 μF, although really high values like these are not found on simple low power circuits. Single number and double number values are more common, e.g., 2.2 or 10—and could be confused with pF in the absence of any symbol. Normally, however, large whole number values usually refer to picofarads and are unlikely to be given in a circuit drawing without the correct symbol following, i.e. (pF).

The prefix m means milli, or 1/1000th while μ means micro, or 1/1,000,000th. However, even large capacitor values are never quoted in millifarads (mF). So if mF (or m) does appear on a circuit drawing, it almost certainly means μF (microfarads).

In the circuit diagrams in this book, where capacitor values are given in a drawing, a capacitor value (number) *without* a following symbol should be read as microfarads (μF). Where capacitor values are in picofarads the numerical value is followed by pF.

PRACTICAL NOTES ON USING COMPONENTS

The usual type of resistor used in transistor circuits is the carbon resistor, made from carbon film. These are available in various sub-types.

☐ *Micro*—the smallest, and usually with a ⅛ watt rating
☐ *Miniature*—usually with a ¼ watt rating
☐ *Standard*—usually with a ½ watt rating
☐ *Power*—with a 1 watt rating

Unless you are dealing with a circuit carrying unusually high power, a micro, miniature, or standard carbon film resistor will usually be quite suitable.

Other types of resistor are:

☐ *Metal film resistors*—with more stable operating characteristics than carbon resistors, but more expensive. You might want to use them in critical circuits. Thin film type usually have ratings from 1/10 to 1/5-watt. Thick film resistors have a 1/2-watt power rating.
☐ *Metal oxide resistors*—more stable still, and far less likely to be damaged by excessive heat when soldering. Normally have a ½-watt rating but are expensive and not readily available in the same range of values as carbon resistors.

□ *Wire-wound resistors*—for very low values (i.e., less than 10 ohms), and also for circuits carrying high power. Ratings may range up to 25 watts or more, depending on value.

For quick reference here is a complete list of individual resistor values available (but not necessarily in all *types* of resistors).

Ohms	Kilohms (thousands of ohms)	Megohms (millions of ohms)
10	1K	1M
12	1.2K	1.2M
15	1.5K	1.5M
18	1.8K	1.8M
22	2.2K	2.2M
27	2.7K	2.7M
33	3.3K	3.3M
39	3.9K	3.9M
47	4.7K	4.7M
56	5.6K	5.6M
68	6.8K	6.8M
82	8.2K	8.2M
100	10K	10M
120	12K	12M
150	15K	15M
180	18K	18M
220	22K	22M
270	27K	27M
330	33K	33M
390	39K	39M
470	47K	47M
560	56K	56M
680	68K	68M
820	82K	82M

"NONSTANDARD" COMPONENT VALUES

Sometimes in a circuit diagram you will find a value given for a resistor or a capacitor that is not available, i.e., is a nonstandard value. This is usually because the required value has been *calculated* and quoted as such rather than adjusted to the nearest *practical* value available. No problem—just use the nearest standard value up *or* down. Either should work.

DIODE EQUIVALENTS

Since diodes also commonly appear in transistor circuits the following list of diode equivalents will be useful. The diode type in the right-hand column is a direct replacement for the type shown in the left-hand column (but not necessarily the other way around).

Diode type	Equivalent
BA100	BAX16
BA145	BY206
BA148	BY206
BAY38	BAX16
BY100	IN4006
DD000	IN4001
DD001	IN4002
DD003	IN4003
DD006	IN4004
IGP7	OA90
ISJ50	OA200
ISJ150	OA202
OA70	OA90
OA73	OA90
OA79	AA119
OA81	OA91
OA85	OA95
ZS170	IN4001
ZS171	IN4002
ZS172	IN4003
ZS174	IN4004
ZS175	IN4005
ZS178	IN4006
ZS270	IN5400
ZS271	IN5401
ZS272	IN5402
ZS274	IN5404
ZS276	IN5406

GETTING THE POLARITY RIGHT

Transistors must always be connected the "right way around" in a circuit, which means correctly identifying the emitter, base, and collector leads. Also observe that the polarity of connection (which governs the direction of current flow through the transistor) is the opposite way around in a PNP type to a NPN type. If a transistor is connected the wrong way the circuit will not work, and the transistor itself may well be damaged. So, as well as making sure that the emitter, base, and collector leads are correctly connected; be equally sure that the battery providing the supply voltage is also connected the right way.

For higher values of capacitance, *electrolytic capacitors* are the common choice (and in some cases the only choice). These also have a definite polarity and must be connected the right way—the + side marked on the capacitor to positive as far as the dc supply voltage is concerned *at that point* in the circuit.

Normally the + side of a capacitor is marked on the circuit drawing where an electrolytic capacitor is called for. If not, and you are using an electrolytic capacitor at that point, check which is the + side of the circuit at that point. It is not always easy to do this. If in doubt, a way out is to complete the circuit, connect to battery and—if the circuit does not work—check the actual polarity at each electrolytic with a voltmeter. If this does not agree with the + side of the capacitor, reconnect it the correct way.

Diodes are another circuit component which must be connected the right way. The + side is normally marked with a red dot or red ring and corresponds to the vertical bar side of the diode symbol in the circuit diagram. Confusion can arise because this side of the diode may be marked (or referred to) as the cathode, or marked with a "k" for cathode, which would seem to be the *negative* side for connection. It is not. However, getting the polarity right is quite easy. If the circuit does not work, just reverse the diode connections and see if that solves the problem.

In many circuits, you can check to see if a diode connected the wrong way is the cause of the circuit not working. Simply short across the diode. If the circuit now works, the diode is connected the wrong way.

Variable capacitors are another component which should be connected the right way, although they will usually work either way. The correct way is with the frame connected to the grounded side of the circuit.

IF A CIRCUIT DOES NOT WORK

The most common cause of a circuit not working is a wrong connection somewhere, so check all connections through against the circuit diagram both during and *after* assembly of the circuit. Even experts frequently make connection mistakes.

The chances of a component itself being faulty are far less—but of course it can happen. If you do suspect a component is faulty, substitute it with a replacement. If that still does not work, almost certainly you have a wrong connection or a *wrong component value*. It is very easy again to make mistakes in reading the color code to identify resistor values. So, again, recheck your resistor values against the color code before you actually connect each resistor into the circuit. Until thoroughly familiar with the color code it is a good idea to *write out* the resistor colors against each resistor on the circuit diagram.

Chapter 4

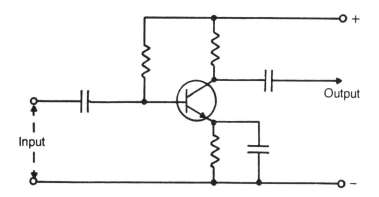

What a Single Transistor Can Do

The variety of working circuits which can be produced around a single transistor is virtually endless. One could start with a "complete" radio receiver, for instance, which requires no battery power at all. This, of course, is the well-known *crystal receiver*, normally based on a germanium diode detector.

The classic circuit is shown in Fig. 4-1. L1 is a proprietary antenna tuning coil wound on a ferrite slab, and C1 is a matching variable capacitor (either 400 or 500 pF). Virtually any diode will do, and the only other circuit component is capacitor C2 connected across the output. Phones must be of high impedance type (headphones or earpiece). An external aerial and a good physical earth connection are essential for satisfactory performance.

The same circuit will work as well, or even better, using nearly any rf germanium transistor. Suggested types are 2N370, 2N371, and 2N3325 or equivalents. Only the base and emitter leads of the transistor are connected into the circuit (replacing the diode). The collector lead of the transistor is ignored. Also it does not matter which way round the transistor is connected. However, this is wasting the full potential of the transistor. It can be made to act as a detector and amplifier in the simple circuit shown in Fig. 4-2. This time a battery is required (which can be anything from 1.5 to 9 volts), and the connections of the transistor are important. Those shown are for any PNP type.

It may be possible to get working results with even fewer

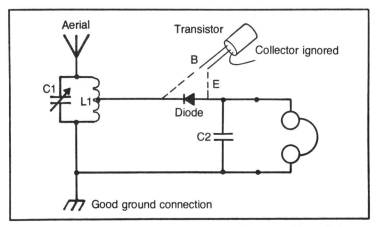

Fig. 4-1. Basic crystal set works without a battery and can use either a diode or a transistor as a detector.

components. Capacitor C3 may well be omitted for instance (try the receiver with and without). Try also shorting out capacitor C2. If this has no appreciable effect, then C2 can be omitted. You may, in fact, get this simple radio working with just five components—an aerial coil, tuning capacitor, two resistors and a transistor, plus a high impedance earpiece and a battery. Such a circuit can be built

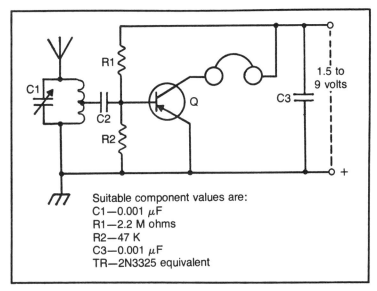

Fig. 4-2. Modified crystal set employing a transistor both as detector and amplifier.

down to a very small size, but you will still need an external aerial and ground for satisfactory reception and reasonable "listening" strength.

AUDIO OSCILLATOR

A single transistor can be used with a transformer to produce a tone generator or audio oscillator—the only other components needed being a couple of resistors and three capacitors. The transformer is a typical transistor radio output transformer. The tone produced can be heard in low impedance phones connected across the output of the transformer using a 3-volt battery; or in a miniature loudspeaker of 16 ohms resistance using a 9-volt battery.

The circuit design is shown in Fig. 4-3. The primary winding of the transformer and capacitor C2 form the tuned circuit giving the oscillation frequency. The center tap on the primary connects to the base of the transistor via the 370 K ohm resistor. Using different values for C2 will alter the tone—higher pitched tone with a lower value of C2, and vice versa. Capacitors C1 and C3 are merely blocking capacitors for direct current in the circuit.

If the circuit does not oscillate, remove the end connections to the primary of the transformer. If this does not produce an audible tone, then the circuit may be oscillating outside the audible fre-

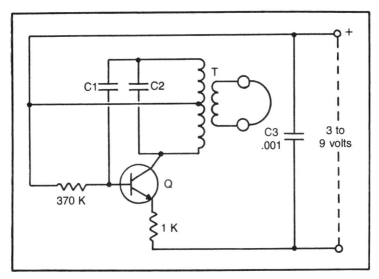

Fig. 4-3. Audio oscillator circuit based on a Motorola HEP S0015 transistor or equivalent. Try 0.01 μF for C1 and 0.02 μF for C2. Resistor values are shown on the diagram. Phones are low impedance type.

quency range. Try higher values for C2 to adjust, and again try removing the transformer connections if necessary.

TRANSISTOR RADIO BOOSTER

Small, inexpensve transistor radios often have low listening volume, particularly on weaker stations, even when listening via a plug-in earpiece. This simple single-transistor circuit will boost earpiece listening levels considerably, so much so, in fact, that a separate volume control is essential.

The circuit is based around an FET transistor—see Fig. 4-4. One side of the circuit is wired to a plug matching the earpiece socket on the transistor radio. This is the input side of the circuit, coupled via capacitor C1, with the potentiometer R1 acting as a potential divider and volume control. An earpiece socket is wired into the output side of the circuit, and a separate 6- or 9-volt battery is required for this circuit, rather than tapping on to the receiver battery. This enables the amplifier to be unplugged from the radio when not required without having also to disconnect leads taken to the receiver battery.

Capacitors C2 and C3 may or may not be required. Try first with C2 connected, then without. If there is no appreciable difference in performance, omit C2. Capacitor C3 should improve the tonal quality of the signal, but since this is usually poor to start with in the case of a miniature transistor radio, it may be an unnecessary elaboration.

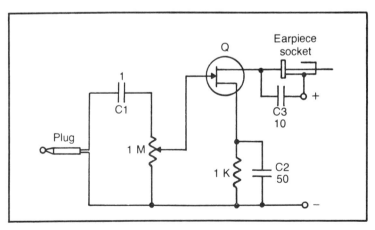

Fig. 4-4. Radio output booster for plugging into earpiece socket on small transistor radios. Earpiece now plugs into socket. Transistor is an FET type 2N3823 or equivalent. Other component values shown on diagram.

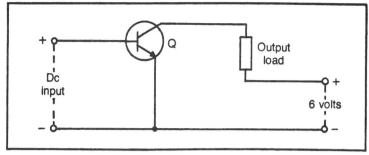

Fig. 4-5. Basic dc amplifier using NPN transistor.

DC AMPLIFIERS

Transistors can also amplify direct current. A basic dc amplifier circuit is shown in Fig. 4-5 which provides *current gain* (i.e., works as a current amplifier). The actual current gain is dependent on the "beta" value of the transistor used, and the value of the resistance load applied to the output (no output current can flow until the output is connected to a resistance load). The resistance of the load must be selected so that the maximum collector current specified for the transistor is not exceeded.

Figure 4-6 shows another type dc amplifier, using an FET. In this case the circuit works as a *voltage amplifier*. The potentiometer R1 acts as a gain control. The value of R2 is chosen so that the maximum drain-to-source voltage of the transistor is not exceeded. Have a look also at the chapter on Amplifiers for other practical amplifier circuits.

SIMPLE STROBOSCOPE

Using an ordinary flashlight bulb for a stroboscope (Fig. 4-7),

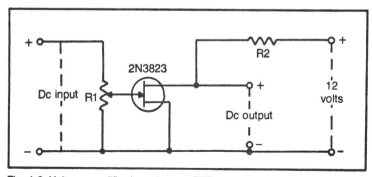

Fig. 4-6. Voltage amplifier based on an FET.

35

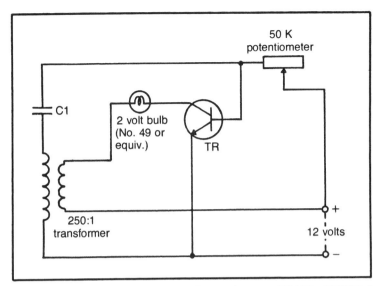

Fig. 4-7. Simple stroboscope using an NPN transistor type BC107 or 2N2712. A suitable value for the blocking capacitor C1 is 50 μF.

instead of a special neon, is quite practical, provided it is accepted that the flashing rate is limited by the inability of a filament to go out and on at high repetition rates. (If it had that ability then electric light bulbs would flicker continuously.)

Maximum flashing rate likely to be achieved is of the order of 20 per second, equivalent to 1200 rpm. If any job calls for a simple low frequency strobe of this order, then this simple circuit will suffice.

It consists of a blocking oscillator with a variable oscillation frequency from about 1 to 25 Hz. The only components involved are one NPN transistor, a miniature 250:1 transformer, a 50 K potentiometer and a blocking capacitor (C1). The bulb is a 2-volt pilot light of the type that draws about 50 milliamps current.

Adjustment of the potentiometer controls the flashing rate. If the circuit does not work as originally connected, reverse the connections to one side of the transformer.

MATCHING TRANSISTORS TO COMPONENTS

With many circuit designs there are no problems about component values required. A particular type or types of transistor is specified, together with actual values for associated resistors and capacitors. Still no particular problems if you cannot get the actual

36

transistor(s) specified but can obtain an equivalent. It should work with the same component values in that circuit. But if you cannot get an equivalent—or perhaps the transistor type and actual component values are not specified at all—it is no good guessing. You have to work out matching component values from the characteristics given for the transistor type you think should do the job.

Check what the circuit is supposed to do, and select a category of transistor to match:

☐ In a switching circuit, select a switching transistor.
☐ In an amplifier circuit, select a small signal amplifier transistor.
☐ For a high power circuit, select a power transistor.

If in doubt about switching and amplifying circuits, select a general purpose transistor. It should work equally well as a switch or amplifier.

The simplest configuration you are likely to find in a circuit is that shown in Fig. 4-8 where resistor R1 establishes the bias necessary for the transistor to work and R_C is the collector load (resistance).

A suitable value for R1 can be calculated directly from the transistor characteristics quoted as h_{te} and the "design" circuit flowing through the emitter I_E. This value is unknown for the moment, but will be equal to the current flowing through the collector (I_C) and the base (I_B). However, I_B will be small relative to I_C, so we can assume I_E is virtually the same as I_C.

Now the transistor characteristics will include a figure for

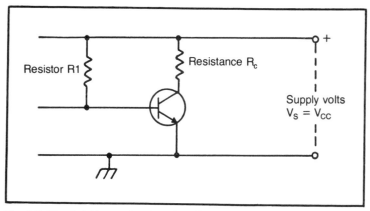

Fig. 4-8. Simplest bias system for a transistor.

37

$I_{C\,max}$—i.e. the maximum permissible collector current. We could safely take half this value as a "design" figure for I_E. The value required for R1 can then be calculated from

$$R1 = \frac{V_s \times h_{te}}{I_E}$$

when V_s is the supply voltage.

Equally the required collector load resistance (R_C) must be such that the specified rate of I_{Cmax} is not exceeded with this current flowing.

Example: A small signal general purpose silicon transistor has specified characteristics of

$$h_{te} = 150\text{-}250$$
$$I_{Cmax} = 100 \text{ mA}$$

Assessing $I_E = \frac{1}{2} \times I_{Cmax} = 50 \text{ mA}$ and $V_s = 9$ volts

$$R = \frac{9 \times 200}{.050}$$

$$= 36000 \text{ ohms}$$

Nearest practical rate available is 33K or 39K, either of which should be suitable.

We also know that to limit I_C to 100 mA, from Ohm's law:

$$resistance = \frac{volts}{amps}$$

$$\text{Thus } R_C = \frac{9}{0.1}$$

$$= 90 \text{ ohms.}$$

Choose a higher preferred value for safety—say 120 or 150 ohms.

A more stable working network for a transistor is shown in Fig. 4-9. Here the bias voltage (V_B) is determined by the values of R1 and R2 and the supply voltage. Resistor R3 works to stabilize the emitter current by producing a voltage drop in the emitter circuit by

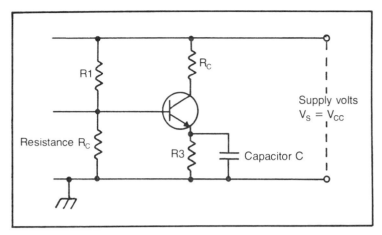

Fig. 4-9. Stabilized bias circuit.

producing a voltage drop in the emitter circuit. This voltage drop needs to be about 1 volt for germanium transistors and up to 3 volts with a silicon transistor. Basically this calls for a fairly large value for R3, but the combined resistance of R2 and R3 in parallel needs to be less than R1 to avoid loss of input signal.

The "design" figure in this case is the base-to-emitter voltage. The transistor specification will give a value for $V_{be\ max}$ (or $V_{eb\ max}$ which is the same thing). Adapt half this value as a design value when you have a complete formula to work with

$$I_E = \frac{R2 \times V_s}{R3\ (R1 + R2)} - \frac{V_{be}}{R3}$$

As a starting point, try a value for R2 which is about four times the impedance of the transistor, and R1 almost twice R2. See what that gives for R3; then recheck that the value of R3 is *less* than

$$\frac{R1 \times R2}{(R1 + R2)\ (1 + h_{ie})}$$

Not exactly a precise method of "designing" a transistor circuit, but it can produce a possible working answer when you are faced with no quoted component values in a circuit.

The capacitor shown in parallel with R3 may or may not be required. Its purpose is to decouple R3 and can be a desirable feature in amplifier circuits. If used it needs to be of high value (10

39

μF at least). It is not necessary in a switching circuit. Even R3 itself is not always necessary with a silicon transistor.

UNIJUNCTION TRANSISTOR CIRCUITS
Unijunction Transistor Metronome

Try this simple circuit (Fig. 4-10) based on a unijunction transistor. With only seven additional components it gives a powerful metronome the beat rate of which can be adjusted over a wide range and works off a 9-volt battery. Any small loudspeaker should be suitable with an impedance of 4 ohms or 8 ohms.

Beat frequency depends on the values of R1 and C1 used. Suitable starting values would be 470K for R1 and 10 μF for C1. To change the frequency substitute 390K or 330K for R1. Alternatively use a 500K pot for R1.

Make sure you get the connections to the unijunction transistor covered. It has three leads like an ordinary transistor (and comes in a similar package). There are two base leads B1 and B2, the third lead being the emitter. Figure 4-10 will help you identify these leads. Incorporate an on-off switch in one of the power lines.

Self-Identifying Calling System

This circuit (Fig. 4-11) uses a unijunction transistor working as

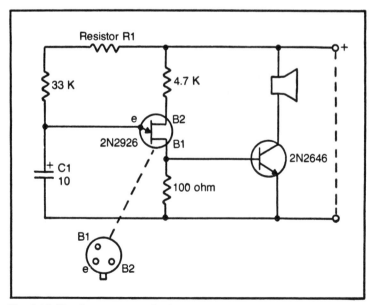

Fig. 4-10. Simple metronome circuit.

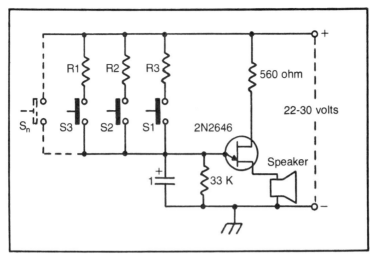

Fig. 4-11. Tone generating circuit.

an oscillator to generate a tone in a small 4-ohm or 8-ohm loudspeaker on closure of switch S1, S2, or S3, etc.

For a "doorbell" system, use pushbutton switches located by each door—e.g., S1 on the front door, S2 on a side door, etc. Use as many switches as you need to cover all required "calling" positions.

Each switch is wired into the circuit via a resistor, i.e., R1, R2, and R3, etc. By using a different value for each resistor the resulting tone sounding in the speaker when a switch is closed will be different for each switch. Thus you can tell by the sound from which position the call is being made.

Choose resistors between 1.8 K and 18 K with as many inter-mediate values as you need, evenly spaced apart. This will then give equal percentage change in tone, viz:

	R1	R2	R3	R4	R5
For 2 calling positions	1.8 K	18 K	—	—	—
For 3 calling positions	1.8 K	5.6 K	18 K	—	—
For 4 calling positions	1.8 K	3.9 K	8.2 K	18 K	—
For 5 calling positions	1.8 K	3.3 K	5.6 K	10 K	18 K

Minimum battery size for satisfactory working is 22 volts.

FLASHER CIRCUITS
Simple LED Flasher

This very simple flasher unit (Fig. 4-12) requires only a 1.5

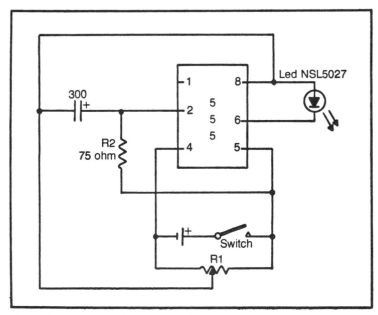

Fig. 4-12. Circuit for a simple LED flasher.

volt battery and will give a flashing rate which can be varied from about 20 Hz downwards to once per second or slower by adjustment of the variable resistor R1. A suitable value for R1 is 5 K but set-up initially in the mid-position.

Current consumption is very low so the on-off switch for the battery can be omitted. Even a small AA size cell should have a life of several weeks left on all the time.

The circuit can be further simplified by omitting R1 and R2 entirely and connecting the capacitor across pins 1 and 2; also connect pin 1 to pin 8. This should give a flashing rate of about once a second. The actual rate can be varied by using different values for the capacitor. Try 200 μF, 250 μF and 350 μF.

Simple Lamp Bulb Flasher

This flasher circuit (Fig. 4-13) will operate a 12 volt lamp bulb with a rating up to 10 watts. The brighter the lamp (i.e., the higher the wattage) the greater the current drawn from the 12-volt supply.

Flashing rate will depend on the tolerances of the resistors used, and also particularly the value of C. Try 10 μF for a start. Use alternative values up or down to alter the flashing rate.

Figure 4-14 is a simpler lamp bulb flash circuit using part of an

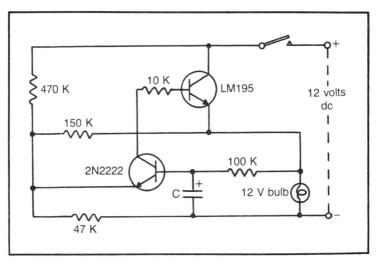

Fig. 4-13. Lamp bulb flasher using two transistors.

LM3909 chip and works off a 6-volt supply. Flashing rate is controlled by the value of C used. Try 400 μF for a start. If you want a different flashing rate, try 380 μF or 300 μF; or 500 μF if you want to adjust the flashing rate the other way.

Intercom

Using an op amp makes it easy to build a two-station intercom requiring only a few additional components. Circuitry will vary

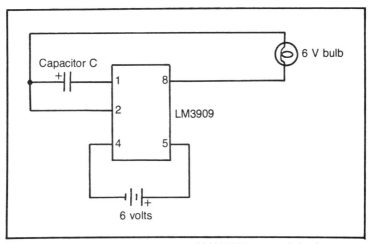

Fig. 4-14. Lamp bulb flasher using part of LM3909 integrated circuit.

43

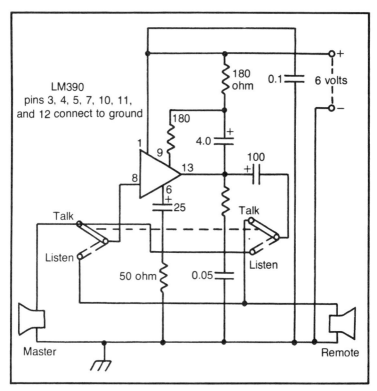

Fig. 4-15. Two-station intercom circuit.

depending on the actual op amp used, but Fig. 4-15 based on a
LM390, is one of the simplest.

Miniature 40-ohm speakers double as microphone /speaker at
both the smaller and remote stations. All circuit components are
built into the master station, with a two wire connection only
required to the remote speaker /microphone. Talk and listen facility
is switchable only at the master station via the gauged switch.

Note that pins 3, 4, 5, 7, 10, 11, and 12 on the op amp, which
are not used, should all be connected to the ground line. This circuit
will work satisfactorily off a 6-volt battery.

Chapter 5

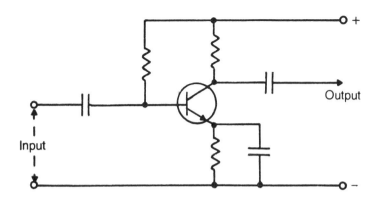

Coupling

Electronic circuits commonly consist of a number of separate stages connected or coupled together. Figure 5-1 illustrates this in block diagram form for three stages. For the sake of making this diagram real, A could be an audio oscillator circuit, B an amplifier, and C a further amplifier stage feeding a loudspeaker. The output side of A has to be coupled to the input of B, and the output of B to the input of C. The output of C is then connected to the loudspeaker.

There are three different ways in which one stage can be coupled to another: direct (i.e., output direct to input), direct, but with a capacitor in the connecting lead, and indirect, through a transformer.

Choice of the type of coupling used is influenced by the characteristics of the circuits involved, as well as the circuit designer's ideas on what is the best method to use in a particular case. Where any of three methods would work, the main thing to remember is that the first will pass both ac and dc, whereas the second and third methods pass only ac from input to output.

Direct coupling is the simplest, and most obvious method. It also eliminates the need for a coupling capacitor or coupling transformer. Besides saving on components, this can also be an advantage from the performance point of view in the case of amplifiers, since any capacitor or inductance in the circuit path will tend to limit the frequency response of the amplifier. Transistor amplifiers, too,

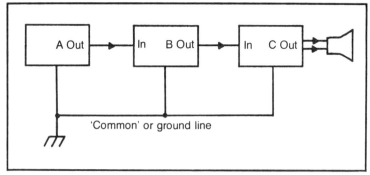

Fig. 5-1. Diagrammatic illustration of 'coupling'.

are particularly suited for direct coupling because a transistor can work as a direct current amplifier.

The basic disadvantage of direct coupling (dc coupling as it is often termed) is, in this case, the problem that the transistor in one stage must be biased by a proportion, or the whole, of the output current of another transistor. In other words, each stage controls the bias of the following stage and any change in the transistor characteristics brought about by heating effects, etc., will also be amplified. This effect is aggravated by the fact that high amplification is already a feature of a dc coupled amplifier. Thus the higher the gain, the more important it is to introduce some satisfactory method of compensating for temperature changes. This can be done by "stabilizing" the transistor circuit, e.g., resistor or capacitor in parallel connection to the emitter in a common-emitter configuration; or the use of a little trick circuitry aimed at the same end.

Figure 5-2 shows the audio end of a simple transistor receiver.

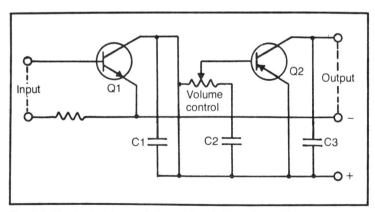

Fig. 5-2. Simple directly coupled 'audio' end of a radio receiver.

46

Q1 is an NPN transistor forming the amplifier stage. Q2 is a PNP transistor forming the output stage. Q1 is biased to near cut-off point so that there is only a small current in the collector, forming the bias for Q2.

Potentiometer R1 is the volume control, but it also acts as a potential divider controlling the bias current. Thus signal and bias increase, or decrease, simultaneously and in step. In the complete circuit, capacitors C1, C2, and C3 are also necessary to bypass the rf components of the amplified signal to ground, leaving only a strong af signal passed to the output.

Direct coupling of amplifier stages like this is commonly employed with transformer coupling at each end, i.e., the input to Q1 is provided by transformer coupling to the preceding stage; and the output from Q2 is transformer-coupled to the loudspeaker. Alternatively, the input side may be capacitor-coupled and the output transformer-coupled.

A capacitor is smaller and cheaper than a transformer and so is commonly preferred for input (or inter-stage) coupling where it is necessary (or desirable) to block the dc voltage from a previous stage. Transistors normally represent a low impedance input and so in order to pass audio frequencies quite high values of capacitance are necessary, e.g., 1 to 100 μF. If only rf is to be passed, lower capacitance values can be used.

The main significance here is that high values of capacitance usually are an indication that is better to use electrolytic capacitors which are polarized, i.e., it is important that they be connected in the circuit the right way round. If not, they will be destroyed.

Capacitor coupling is known as RC coupling since both resistance (R) and capacitance (C) are involved. In amplifier stages the

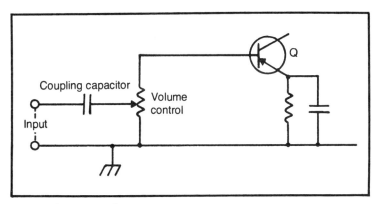

Fig. 5-3. Capacitor or RC coupling.

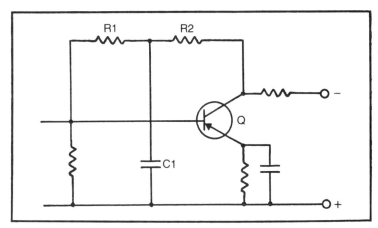

Fig. 5-4. Frequency selective network of the type used in better quality radios. R1, R2 and C1 are three components forming the network.

same necessity for stabilizing the transistor in the following stage applies. Again a potentiometer can be used both as a volume control and current divider to change signal level and bias simultaneously, but stabilizing components are also usually employed in the emitter circuit—see Fig. 5-3.

Transformer coupling has the advantage that it can readily provide a proper impedance match, and thus work with high efficiency. In certain cases only a transformer will provide the necessary impedance match, such as coupling a high impedance output to a low impedance input. A typical example is the use of transformer coupling between a transistor output stage and a low impedance speaker.

The main disadvantage of transformer coupling in an audio circuit is that the impedance will rise with higher frequencies, which can affect the quality of the output. This can be compensated by feeding back a proportion of the collector current from the transistor output to the transistor base. With the correct amount of feedback this has the effect of controlling the stability of the impedance of the circuit and thus the frequency response. Instead of simple feedback through a single resistor, a frequency-selective network of the type shown in Fig. 5-4 would be used for this purpose.

48

Chapter 6

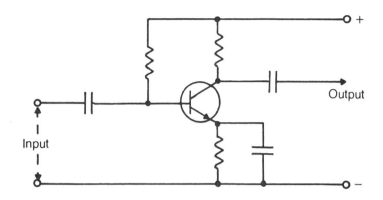

Amplifiers

The basic circuit for a PNP transistor af amplifier is shown in Fig. 6-1. This would normally be RC coupled at the input and output (see previous chapter on Coupling). The dc base bias is produced by the potential divider formed by R1 and R2, and the emitter resistor R3. R3 and C2 also stabilize the circuit. R4 is the collector load; and C1 and C3 the input and output coupling capacitors, respectively. These should be 1 μF or larger value.

Actual component values depend on the type of transistor used; also the gain depends on the characteristics of the transistor. The caption summarizes suitable component values to match common types of transistor.

Figure 6-2 shows the corresponding circuit for a NPN silicon transistor. The particular advantages offered by this type of transistor are higher impedance, lower collector current, better frequency response and less susceptibility to temperature (see also Chapter 1 on transistors). Again typical matching component values are given in the caption. Coupling capacitor values (C1 and C3) would need to be somewhat higher than before, e.g., 9 or 10 μF.

Gain from either simple amplifier stage can be up to 100 or more, depending on the characteristics of the transistor used. If high gain is not the primary aim, the bypass capacitor C2 can, with advantage, be omitted on the NPN circuit of Fig. 6-2. This will introduce negative feedback, increasing the *quality* of the amplifier at the expense of roughly halving the gain. This little trick increases

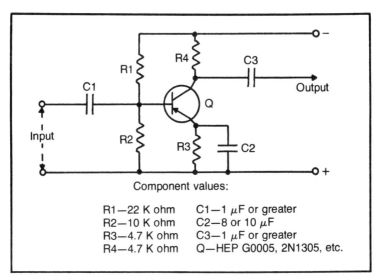

Fig. 6-1. PNP transistor amplifier.

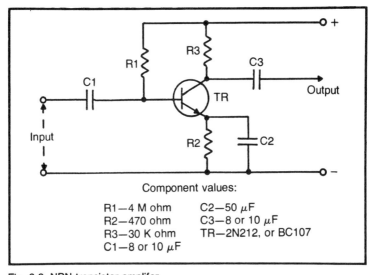

Component values:

R1—22 K ohm   C1—1 µF or greater
R2—10 K ohm   C2—8 or 10 µF
R3—4.7 K ohm   C3—1 µF or greater
R4—4.7 K ohm   Q—HEP G0005, 2N1305, etc.

input impedance, reduces distortion and improves the linearity of the amplifier.

To complete the picture of basic circuits, Fig. 6-3 shows an FET amplifier. The chief characteristic of this type of amplifier is a very high input impedance, but relatively low gain. Practically any type of FET will work as an amplifier in this configuration, the

Component values:

R1—4 M ohm   C2—50 µF
R2—470 ohm   C3—8 or 10 µF
R3—30 K ohm   TR—2N212, or BC107
C1—8 or 10 µF

Fig. 6-2. NPN transistor amplifer.

50

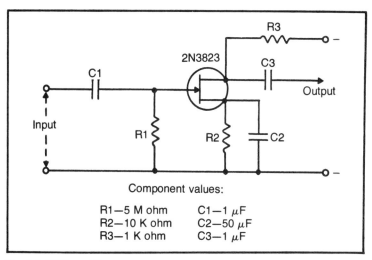

Fig. 6-3. FET amplifier.

component values shown matching a 2N3823 or near equivalent. For matching purposes the input impedance is equal to the value of R1, and the output impedance approximately the same as R2. R2 can be adjusted down (or even omitted entirely) to produce what is, in effect, an impedance converter (high input impedance stage with low output impedance).

ADDING A VOLUME CONTROL

The most direct type of volume control which can be used with the basic circuits of Fig. 6-1 or Fig. 6-2 is a potentiometer inserted in the input side—Fig. 6-4. This then directly controls the strength

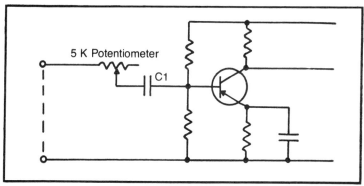

Fig. 6-4. Using a potentiometer as a volume control on the input side to an amplifier.

of the input signal, and thus the output (which equals input signal strength multiplied by gain). A suitable potentiometer value would be 5 K.

In the case of the FET amplifier the potentiometer can replace R1. Here the value required would be of the order of 10 megohms.

CASCADED AMPLIFIERS

Any of the three basic circuits described can be cascaded with other stages of the same type, each stage providing a further gain—Fig. 6-5. There are practical limits to the gain which can be achieved in this manner as, with increasing gain, there will come a point where the output signal is clipped and distortion appears. Also each succeeding stage will suffer a voltage drop and thus an effective loss of voltage gain. The FET amplifier is the exception in this respect.

TUNED AMPLIFIERS

Tuned amplifiers can be one of two types: *Bandpass*—meaning that they "peak" at a particular frequency and so pass a particular frequency band, and *Bandstop*—meaning that they are tuned to reject a particular frequency if present and so eliminate it from the output signal.

These particular circuits may also be described as *filters*, i.e., bandpass filters or bandstop filters (see Fig. 6-6).

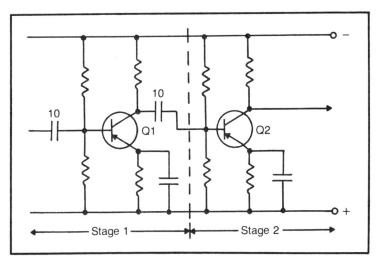

Fig. 6-5. Two identical amplifiers coupled together or cascaded. Output from the first stage is input to the second stage.

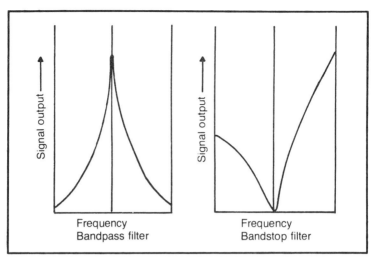

Fig. 6-6. Characteristics of the two basic filter circuits.

The tuned amplifier circuit of Fig. 6-7 is a bandpass type. The resonant circuit comprising L1 and C2 is tuned to the bandpass required. This circuit, together with C3 forms a negative feedback path from collector to base of the transistor, except at resonant frequency. In other words, at all other frequencies the feedback present reduces the gain of the transistor to virtually negligible

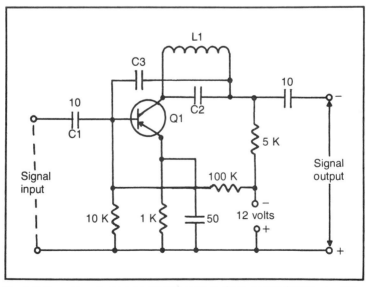

Fig. 6-7. Tuned bandpass type amplifier circuit, Q1 is a HEP G0005 or equiv.

53

proportions. The resonant frequency content of the input signal, however, provides no feedback, and so this signal is passed by the amplifier with full gain.

The circuit is adjusted by varying the inductance. L1 is a choke wound on a former with an iron dust core. Actual inductance and the corresponding value of C2 are chosen to cover the resonant frequency required. The resonant circuit is then adjusted to peak at the specific frequency by adjustment of the dust core.

Exactly the same effect could be obtained from a variable capacitor for C2 and a fixed inductance for L1, peaking to the frequency required by adjusting C1. However, this will give broader tuning than an adjustable inductance, so for sharply peaked tuning the original circuit is preferred.

Suitable values for L1 and C2 can be calculated from the standard "tuned circuit" formula:

$$\text{Resonant frequency (kHz)} = \frac{1}{2\pi \sqrt{LC}}$$

where L = inductance in henries and C = capacitance in farads.

Since it is the values of L and C that have to be determined, it is easier to start by reworking the formula:

$$\sqrt{LC} = \frac{1}{2\pi \times f}$$

$$\text{i.e., } LC = \frac{1}{40 \, f^2} \quad \text{(approx)}$$

where f = resonant frequency in kHz.

Suitable values for L and C can then be obtained by guesstimating one value and then calculating the corresponding value for the other. This can be done several times, if necessary, to end up with realistic matching values.

Example: resonant or pass frequency required is 1000 Hz. A 5 henry (adjustable) choke is "guesstimated."

Substituting in the formula:

$$5 \times C = \frac{1}{40 \times (1)^2} \text{ or } C = \frac{1}{200}$$
$$= 0.005 \, \mu F$$
$$= 500 \, pF$$

BANDSTOP FILTER

The bandstop amplifier employs a similar resonant circuit in what appears an almost identical circuit—Fig. 6-8. However, in this case the negative feedback is present only at the resonant or "stop" frequency. All other frequencies in the input signal are passed with normal amplifier gain. In practice the filter performance will be of the "matched" type, the characteristic of which is an LC tuned bandstop amplifier (as shown in Fig. 6-6).

RF AND I-F AMPLIFIERS

Rf amplifiers are again similar in basic layout, the transistor used being an rf type rather than an af type. Rf and i-f (intermediate frequency) amplifiers are primarily concerned with radio circuits, which are outside the scope of this particular book.

DC AMPLIFIERS

Amplifiers can also be used to boost, or provide gain, from purely direct current inputs as well as af or rf signals. They can be designed to boost voltage (dc voltage amplifiers) or boost current (dc current amplifiers).

A very simple dc voltage amplifier is shown in Fig. 6-9 based on an FET. Using a 2N3823 FET (or equivalent) and a battery voltage of 12 for powering the circuit, there will be a standing voltage of about 0.6 developed across the output terminals.

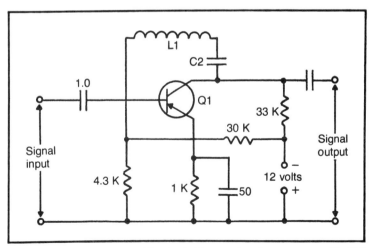

Fig. 6-8. Tuned bandstop amplifier circuit. The transistor is same type as Fig. 6-7. Other component values shown on diagram.

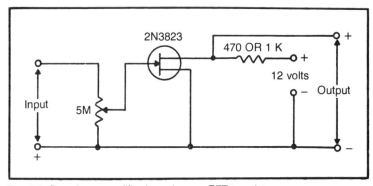

Fig. 6-9. Dc voltage amplifier based on an FET transistor.

Any small dc voltage applied to the input will result in the open circuit output voltage rising to the gain of the amplifier (about 5 in this configuration). Thus applying 1.5 volts to the input, output open circuit voltage would rise to about $5 \times 1.5 = 7.5$ volts. A 3 volt input would give an output voltage of about 15 volts—the limit to the input voltage being the maximum drain-to-source voltage the transistor can take. In this respect the value of R2 is fairly important. A value of 470 ohms would be satisfactory for input voltages up to 1.5, and 1 K for voltages up to 4.5.

It is also possible with this circuit to adjust the actual output open circuit voltage for a maximum drain to any designed level for any given input voltage. Simply replace the 470 or 1 K resistor with a 1 K ohm potentiometer and adjust to set the output voltage.

A conventional transistor is basically a *current amplifier* and again can be worked in a simple circuit of the type shown in Fig. 6-10 as a dc current amplifier. Battery power has to be applied to the circuit, as well as a dc input voltage. A silicon transistor works best as this has an inherently low static collector current and is not greatly affected by temperature. The maximum output current

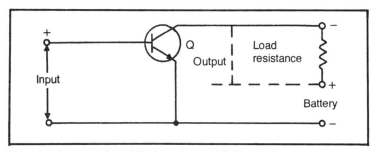

Fig. 6-10. Dc current amplifier based on an NPN transistor.

56

must, however, be kept within the working limits of the transistor by a suitable value for the load resistance. For high current amplifiers, a power transistor must be used.

The amplification produced by this circuit is approximately equal to the current flowing in the base circuit multiplied by the current gain characteristic value of the transistor used. The power gain is very much higher.

TELEPHONE AMPLIFIER

This is a straightforward four stage amplifier (Fig. 6-11) circuit with push-pull output feeding a miniature 4- to 8-ohm speaker and capable of producing excellent volume, worked off a 4.5- or 6-volt battery. A volume control is included in the circuit. For convenience this can be of combined switch and potentiometer type, so that this component can act both as an on—off switch for the battery and volume control for the circuit once switched on.

To connect to the telephone a magnetic (inductive) pick-up is used, attached to the outside of the telephone case. It is illegal to connect directly into a telephone circuit in Britain. The best position for the pick-up coil must be found by trial-and-error. Usually it will be on the right-hand side of a modern hand set unit (not the part you hold), approximately level with the top of the dial and mid-way down the side.

Proprietary pick-up coils are encapsulated and fitted with a rubber suction cup for holding them in position. This is usually found to drop off frequently, so once the best position has been found, secure with a dab of contact adhesive, pressing firmly in place.

RECEIVER PREAMP

A radio frequency amplifier can be used as a preamplifier to boost the signal strength received by an ordinary radio receiver. This can be specially useful in areas of low signal strength where a pocket transistor radio is often inadequate to cope because it is lacking in sensitivity, and also for improving the *selectivity* of any set (i.e., making it capable of separating broadcast stations).

The rf preamp is a standard basic circuit (Fig. 6-12) with the addition of a tuned circuit L1 and C2 in the collector circuit. Components used here are exactly the same as in any radio receiver, i.e., a standard aerial tuning coil on a Ferrite rod or "loopstick" and a 365 pF variable capacitor. Power for the preamp circuit can be tapped directly from the receiver circuit to avoid using a separate battery.

Output of the preamp is capacity-coupled direct to the receiver

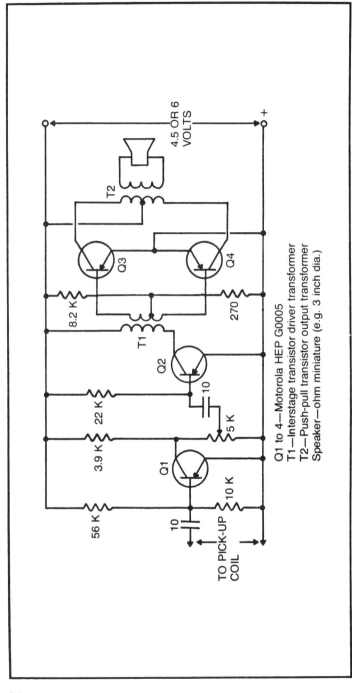

Q1 to 4—Motorola HEP G0005
T1—Interstage transistor driver transformer
T2—Push-pull transistor output transformer
Speaker—ohm miniature (e.g. 3 inch dia.)

Fig. 6-11. Telephone amplifier circuit.

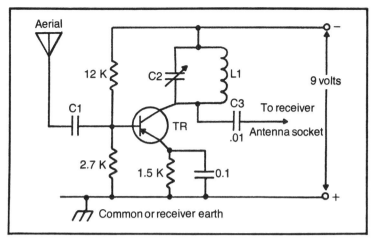

Fig. 6-12. Receiver preamplifier based on a standard tuned circuit (antenna coil L1 and 365 pF variable capacitor C2). Suitable transistor types are 2N1303, HEP G0003.

aerial socket, if one is fitted. If not, take this connection via C3 to the end of this circuit which is connected to the common ground of the receiver circuit. It is necesary to identify this common ground. connection anyway as the ground connection of the preamps also has to be connected to receiver ground. Do *not* assume that this will be the battery + terminal in the receiver circuit. It could be the other way around.

The preamp may work satisfactorily without an external antenna connection. In this case C1 and the aerial shown on the circuit diagram can be omitted. Much better results, and more stations will be brought in at good listening strength, if an external aerial is connected to the preamp. Experiment with different values of C1 for best results, e.g., from, say, 100 pF up to 0.01 μF, or use a 500 pF trimmer capacitor. You will find that experimenting with different capacitor values here (or using a trimmer) will *either* improve selectivity (or separation of the stations) *or* volume of signal. You cannot have it both ways!

SIMPLE OP-AMP CIRCUITS

The operational amplifier or op amp is a highly versatile device produced in numerous configurations in a simple IC package. While there are numerous basic circuits for simple op amps, associated discrete (i.e., additional) component values are tied to the actual construction of individual op amps, so working circuits must be

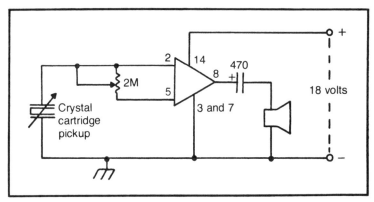

Fig. 6-13. Power amplifier for a crystal cartridge.

based around specific types and their specific allocation of pin numbers.

Crystal Cartridge Power Amplifier

The LM380 is an extremely useful op amp capable of developing 2.5 watts rms when driven by a high output crystal pickup, using only two additional components—a 2 MΩ pot with log characteristics and a 470 μF capacitor, as shown in Fig. 6-13. The device has a fixed gain of 34 dB, with input variable by the pot, which therefore acts as a volume control. The other useful characteristics of this op amp are that the output is short-circuit proof, also the device itself incorporates its own heat sink.

With just two more components it is possible also to incorporate tone control in this circuit—Fig. 6-14. Note that only 5 pins are used in connecting this particular op amp (the actual device has 14 pins, but the other nine are unused in these circuits).

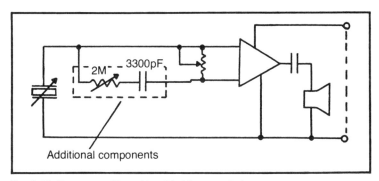

Fig. 6-14. Power amplifier with added tone control.

Stereo Amplifier

A large number of IC devices are produced as stereo amplifiers incorporating two separate op amps in a single chip. This can greatly reduce the number of components required to build a complete stereo amplifier for radios, cassette players, car stereo systems, etc. The example chosen here is the LM377 which gives an output of 2 watts per channel into 8-ohm or 16-ohm speakers on a supply voltage of 10-18 V. The IC circuit also has a good degree of protection against thermal or current overload, making it a good general purpose choice.

The complete stereo amplifier circuit is shown in Fig. 6-15. One stereo channel is connected as input to pin 6 and the other stereo channel to pin 9, with stereo outputs from pins 2 and 13,

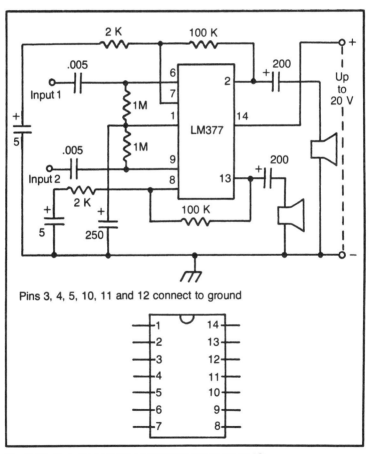

Pins 3, 4, 5, 10, 11 and 12 connect to ground

Fig. 6-15. Two-channel stereo amplifier based on an IC.

respectively. Pins 7 and 8 are the feedback connections to the separate op amps. Other pin connections can be followed from the diagram (but note that the pins are not shown in the same order as the pins actually appear on the IC—see pinout diagram). Note that all the unused pins, 3, 4, 5, 10, 11, and 12 are connected to ground.

Operating voltage applied to pin 14 (plus voltage connection) and ground can be anything up to 20 V. Input voltage, via the stereo channels, can be anything between 4 mV and 80 mV. Current drain at 1.5 watts power output per channel is about 430 mA.

You will find many other ICs incorporating two separate op amps to work as stereo amplifiers in a similar, if not identical circuit. However pin numbering may differ appreciably.

Check the pin numbering for any other dual-op amp against the following:

Pin Labelled	Connects to pin number position on diagram (Fig. 6-15)
input 1	6
input 2	9
bias	1
output 1	2
output 2	13
supply V+	14
ground	ground

Note, however, that different external component values may be needed (though you could try those given for LM3777 in the absence of any information on this subject). Also the feedback connections (pins 2 to 7 and 13 to 8 on the circuit diagram) may need a capacitor connected in parallel across the resistor (try 0.2 μF).

Multivibrator/Oscillator

This free-running multivibrator circuit (Fig. 6-16) or oscillator works with a positive grounded supply, using a LM301A op amp. The frequency of oscillation is governed by the value of C used, e.g., making C = 0.01 μF should give an oscillation frequency of 100 Hz. Decreasing the value of C will give increasing higher frequencies up to about 1 kHz or more before the circuit no longer works. Increasing the value of C will give lower frequencies of oscillation.

Remember that capacitor values are only nominal and not exact, so two different capacitors of the same nominal value could

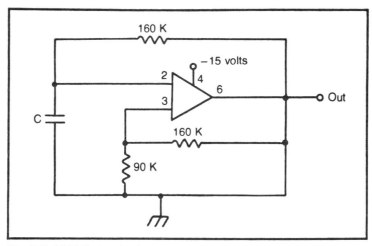

Fig. 6-16. Multivibrator circuit.

well give different oscillation frequencies in this circuit. Use polyester types for preference.

Simple IC Oscillator/Flasher

Here is a very simple oscillation circuit (Fig. 6-17) that will deliver pulses of 2 V through an external load when powered by a 1.5 V battery. It is based on the LM3909 IC, which is basically

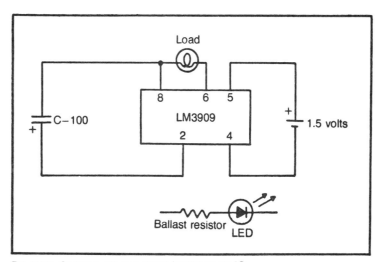

Fig. 6-17. Oscillator/flasher circuit based on an IC.

designed as an LED flasher, using an LED with a high rated forward current. Flashing rate is calculated by the values of the capacitor C, which should be of the order of 100 μF to start with. Adjust this value up or down to vary the flashing rate. Also, for the best results, select an LED with a high rated forward voltage current, otherwise connect a ballast resistor of 100 ohms in series with the LED. If the LED is too dim, try it without the resistor.

Instead of an LED you can try an ordinary 2.5 V light bulb for the load, or even a small 8-ohm loudspeaker to give a "sound" rather than a "light" signal. It should also work both an LED and a small speaker connected in series. Adjust the value of C up or down as necessary to get the circuit working.

Variable Current and Voltage Regulators

A number of ICs are designed as adjustable current and voltage regulators. They will work in either mode, but require different external circuitry and normally incorporate current limiting, power limiting, and thermal overload protection built into them. That makes them virtually indestructable.

Figure 6-18 shows such a device used in a variable current regulator circuit. Output current is variable from a minimum (determined by the internal resistance of the IC) up to the maximum rating from the device (2 amps in this case), via the variable resistor. Note that current regulation is achieved with a small loss

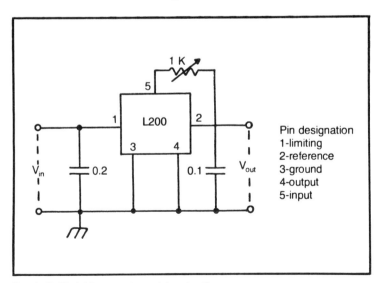

Fig. 6-18. Variable current regulator circuit.

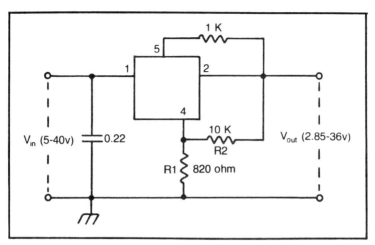

Fig. 6-19. Variable voltage regulator circuit.

of voltage. Figure 6-19 shows the same device used in a variable voltage regulator current. In this case (with the L200 device) the output voltage value is given by:

$$V_{out} = 2.77 \quad \left(1 + \frac{R2}{R1} \right).$$

Chapter 7

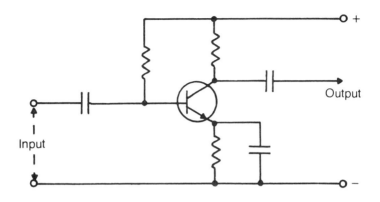

Oscillators

An oscillator is usually part of a circuit, although it can be used as a frequency generator for individual application. The working of an oscillator circuit is basically that of an amplifier when part of the output energy is returned to the input to produce a cyclic, or oscillating, change in the amplifier conduction. These changes can occur at radio frequencies (rf oscillator) or at lower audio frequencies (af oscillator). In the latter case the oscillator generates a tone which can be heard, in a suitable output circuit.

The basic elements of an oscillator circuit are: an amplifier, a feedback arrangement to provide oscillation, and a frequency-selective system to stabilize the oscillation at a particular frequency.

A source of power is also necessary to replace losses in the circuit.

One of the three basic configurations can be used in a transistor oscillator circuit—common-emitter, common-base or common-collector. The common-emitter oscillator is usually preferred as the impedance match in the circuit is not at all critical and there is thus a wide range of tolerance as regards component values and individual transistor characteristics before the oscillator will not work.

A basic circuit of this type is shown in Fig. 7-1. L1 and L2 are transformer coils, the output through L2 inducing a corresponding current in L1 which is fed back to the base of the transistor. L1 is

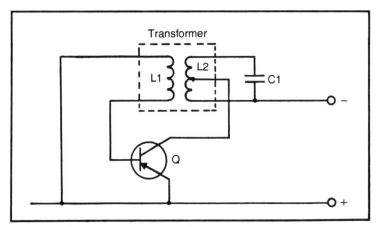

Fig. 7-1. Basic common-emitter oscillator.

sometimes called a "tickler" coil. L2 and C1 provide the frequency-selective system, or tuned circuit, with both L1 and L2 designed to give maximum feedback at the resonant frequency of this circuit. This resonant frequency can be tunable, e.g., by making L2 tunable (via an iron dust core); or C1 tunable (e.g., using a variable capacitor). At the same time the values of L1 and the tapped portion of L2 provide the impedance match for the transistor.

A working circuit of this type is shown in Fig. 7-2 based on a transistor as the amplifier. Component values given are for a range of oscillation frequencies from about 3-10 kHz (tunable by the 365-500 pF variable capacitor), i.e., this is an af oscillator. Dif-

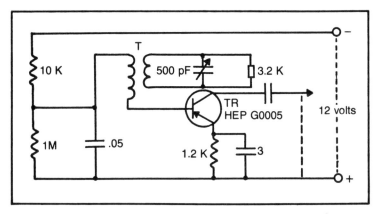

Fig. 7-2. Working circuit for a common-emitter oscillator: TR is a G0005; or equivalent. T is a 40:1 miniature transformer with a secondary inductance of about 5 mH.

ferent component values would be needed for an rf oscillator. As shown, the circuit would be useful as a signal generator for aligning a superhet receiver. Optimum performance as a signal generator would be achieved by replacing the variable capacitor C1 with a fixed capacitor of 0.5 μF, when the (fixed) frequency of oscillation should be approximately 10 kHz.

HARTLEY OSCILLATOR

It is possible to use one winding of a transformer for both the tuned circuit and feedback. The other coil of the transformer can then provide an identically coupled output. This is a Hartley type oscillator, a working circuit for which is shown in Fig. 7-3. Capacitor C3 can be fixed (e.g., 0.02 μF value would give a resonant frequency of approximately 2000 Hz with a typical transformer) or variable. In the latter case a variable capacitor of 50-200 pF would give a wide variation in signal tone generated in the audio range. Connection of low impedance phones to the second coil (output) of the transformer would enable the signal to be heard without further amplification being necessary. In other words, this circuit is a complete "tone" generator.

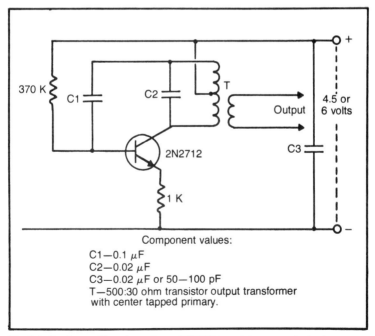

Fig. 7-3. Hartley oscillator based on a 2N2712 transistor, or equivalent.

69

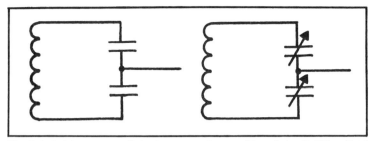

Fig. 7-4. Colpitts type oscillator taps capacitance of tuned circuit. Either fixed (left) or variable capacitors (right) can be used.

There is nothing critical about this circuit and it should work with a variety of similar (near-equivalent) transistor types; or with other af transistors with modified values for R1 and R2. The only thing likely to go wrong (apart from a component being faulty) is that the connections of L1 may be the wrong way round, i.e., the wrong half is connected for feedback. Thus if the circuit does not work, simply reverse the connection of L1, which should cure the trouble.

COLPITTS OSCILLATOR

The Colpitts type oscillator is basically similar but taps the capacitance side of the tuned circuit instead of the coil (inductance). In practice this requires two capacitors in the tuned circuit, which may be fixed or variable—Fig. 7-4.

For a simple af oscillator, this circuit may be simplified by using the phones themselves as the source of inductance in the tuned circuit, eliminating the need for a transformer or even a

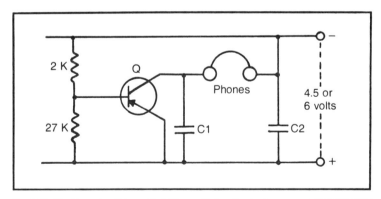

Fig. 7-5. Working circuit for a Colpitts oscillator. Typical component values are C1 = 720 pF and C2 = 125 μF for phones of 2,000 ohms resistance. Q is a HEP G0005.

separate coil. The working circuit then simplifies to that shown in Fig. 7-5.

The equivalent inductance of the phones used, and the values of C1 and C2, determine the oscillation frequency. For phones of approximately 2000 ohms resistance, values of C1 = 250 pF and C2 = 125 μF should result in a tone frequency of approximately 1000 Hz. Decreasing the values of C1 and C2 will raise the frequency; and raising the values of C1 and C2 will lower the tone frequency. A 1:10 ratio should be present between C1 and C2 for satisfactory working of the circuit, so this naturally precludes the use of variable capacitors for C1 and C2, which might appear at first sight a logical solution for tone adjustment.

Circuits of the Colpitts type are used in the morse code sender circuits (see later), as being about the simplest that can be devised for this particular application.

PHASE-SHIFT OSCILLATOR

A phase-shift oscillator circuit works on the basis of providing a 180 degree phase shift between output and input to initiate oscillation. This phase shift can be accomplished with a combination of resistance and capacitance providing an RC (resistance-capacitance) network.

A working circuit of this type is shown in Fig. 7-6. The RC network components are R1, C1, R2, C2, R3, C3, each providing a separate "leg" contributing an equal amount to the phase shift. R3 is made variable to provide adjustment to get the circuit working (i.e.,

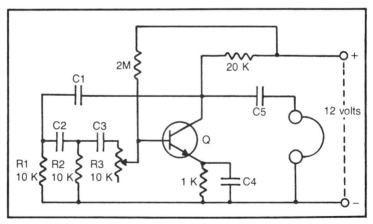

Fig. 7-6. Working circuit of a phase-shift oscillator. Q is an NPN type 2N2646, or CV9695.

to adjust for any differences in the individual characteristics of the transistor specified). Theortically R1, R2, and R3 should have identical values; and also C1, C2, and C3. The tone frequency generated is then equal to:

$$\frac{1,000,000}{20 \times R \times C}$$

where R is in ohms and C is in microfarads.

For a tone frequency of 2000 Hz, suitable values for R1, R2, and R3 would be 10 K; with corresponding values of 0.0025 μF for C1, C2, and C3.

Another type of phase shift network is shown in Fig. 7-7, R1 C1, R2 C2, and R3 C3 again being the three separate legs of the network where each contributes a 60 degree phase shift.

RELAXATION OSCILLATOR

A *unijunction* transistor is, in itself, an amplifying/oscillating device and only a very simple circuit is needed to get it working. In Fig. 7-8, R1 and C1 determine the oscillation frequency. Suitable values are given in the caption. Low impedance phones, or even a small 8-ohm loudspeaker, can be connected directly to the output. In the latter case, if the volume is too low, battery voltage can be increased up to a maximum of 18 volts.

A useful modification to this circuit is to replace R1 with a 10 or

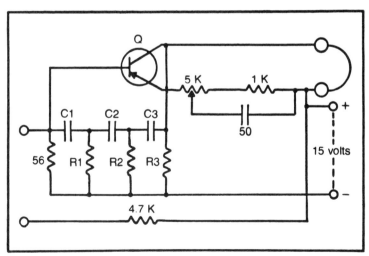

Fig. 7-7. Phase-shift oscillator circuit based on an NKT224, 2N633, 2N60 or AC128 transistor.

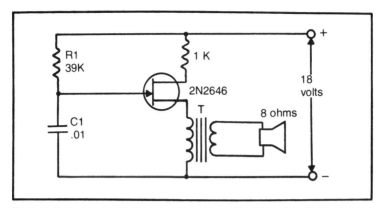

Fig. 7-8. Relaxation oscillator circuit based on a 2N2646 unijunction transistor. T1 is a general-purpose transistor output transformer.

25 K potentiometer and a fixed resistor of 22 K in series. Adjustment of the variable resistor will vary the tone produced. It is necessary to have a fixed resistance left in the circuit in the event of the potentiometer being tuned to zero resistance position in order to limit the voltage and current supplied to the emitter of the transistor.

Virtually any type of unijunction transistor should work in this circuit with the component values given. The specific type recommended is the old-time standby 2N2646.

A unijunction transistor has one *emitter* lead and two *base* leads (no collector). The polarity of connection of these two base leads is important.

COMPARING "NOTES"

It is interesting to compare the sound quality of the tones produced by different types of af oscillator circuits. A phase-shift oscillator, for example, will produce a fairly pure tone. A relaxation oscillator will produce a more rasping tone. This is because of the difference in waveforms generated during oscillation. The phase-shift type usually produces a sine wave while the other rasping tone comes from a "peaked" waveform.

LIGHT-OPERATED OSCILLATOR

Although a source of power is essential to keep an oscillator circuit working, the actual amount of power required can be quite small—small enough, that is, to be provided by a light-sensitive device such as the solar cell. Such a circuit requires no battery and can be used as an alarm device, automatically switching on and giving a tone signal when the light-sensitive device is illuminated.

A working circuit is shown in Fig. 7-9 based on any of the general purpose hobbyist devices widely available as the light-sensitive element; and a HEP G0005 transistor as the amplifier. The former take the place of a battery. The transistor is connected on to a Hartley oscillator circuit, the only critical component being the center tapped coil L. This consists of 600 turns of #40 gauge enameled wire wound on a 1½-in. piece of ordinary pencil. A loop is taken out at the center of this winding (at 300 turns) for the center tap connection.

When the photocell, or solar cell, is illuminated by stray light (e.g., sunlight), sufficient power about ½ volt should be generated in the circuit for the tone to be heard in a high impedance earpiece connected directly to the output. To work as a light-operated alarm working a loudspeaker at least one stage of transistor amplification should be added (see chapter on Amplifiers), connected to a step-down transister output transformer. The speaker is then connected to the output of this transformer.

CRYSTAL OSCILLATOR

A crystal oscillates at a specific frequency (or harmonic frequency) determined by its manufacture. Thus a crystal can be used in an oscillator circuit to stabilize the oscillation to work only at the resonant frequency of the crystal, or some harmonic. This principle is used to stabilize transmitter frequencies for model radio control operation, for example, where law permits operation only within a specific (27 and 72 MHz) rf band.

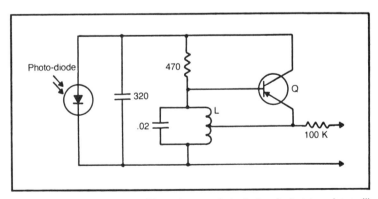

Fig. 7-9. Simple light-operated based on an photodiode. A phototransistor will also work in this circuit.

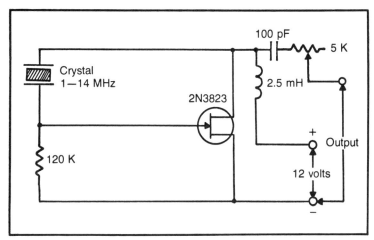

Fig. 7-10. Crystal controlled oscillator based on an FET transistor.

Since an FET provides the simplest type of oscillator the circuit shown (Fig. 7-10) demonstrates 100 pF crystal control, using the absolute minimum of components. This circuit will oscillate only at the fundamental frequency of the crystal, provided the circuit is not overloaded. This means ensuring that the impedance of the output lead is high enough to limit the current to a suitable level. If necessary, connect a 5 K potentiometer in the output as a load control (as shown in the circuit diagram).

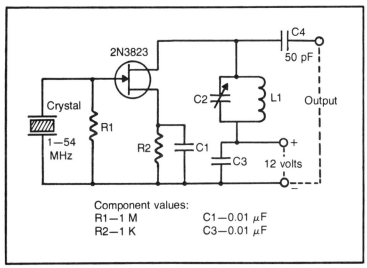

Fig. 7-11. Crystal oscillator circuit with tuned rf output.

Output will be a single frequency oscillation, with the actual frequency dependent only on the resonant frequency of the crystal.

TUNED CRYSTAL OSCILLATOR

This circuit (Fig. 7-11) again used an FET as an oscillator, but is a little more complex, with a number of additional components. Although this circuit oscillates at the crystal frequency, the output is variable for maximum rf signal via C2. C2 and L1 form a tuned circuit, the resonant frequency of which must be the same as that of the crystal, i.e., the values of C2 and L1 are chosen to provide this resonant frequency with the variable range offered by C2.

This circuit is rather more susceptible to the effects of output load than the previous one, as not only can insufficient input load cause dangerous currents to be developed, but even with moderate or high loads giving satisfactory oscillation, the load can detune the resonant circuit L1 and C2, with consequent loss of rf output unless readjusted.

Chapter 8

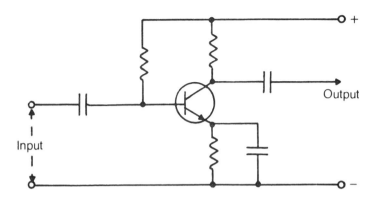

Outputs

In simple audio circuits some amplification of the output is often desirable to boost the signal to good listening level in headphones, rather than having to use a high impedance earpiece. One of the simplest and most efficient output amplifiers to use in this case is the circuit shown in Fig. 8-1 based on an FET. The headphone in this case can be of conventional magnetic type with a coil resistance on the order of 2000 ohms.

The potentiometer R1 acts as a volume control in this output circuit. The tone quality of the phones can also be improved with a capacitor connected in parallel, as shown (C2). In theory, a variable capacitor could be used, but these are not practical at the capacitance values required. Instead capacitors of different values between, say 0.01 and 0.001 μF should be tried, selecting the one which gives the best tone with the headphones used.

Another output problem which can arise is using low impedance phones or speaker; or a low-impedance earpiece fed by a transistor output stage. The latter requires a high impedance to match. The solution in this case is to employ a step-down transformer which acts not only as a coupling between output and phones, but provides a suitable step-down ratio for impedance matching (Fig. 8-2).

Typical values for low-impedance earpieces are:

4 ohm dc resistance (15 ohm impedance at 100 Hz)

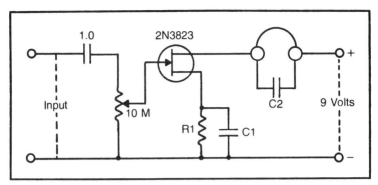

Fig. 8-1. Simple output circuit using FET transistor. Suitable component values are: R1 = 470 ohms, C1 = 50 μF, C2 between 0.01 and 0.001 μF.

14 ohm dc resistance (60 ohm impedance at 100 Hz)
60 ohm dc resistance (250 ohm impedance at 1000 Hz)

Matching transformer step-down ratios to give a nominal output impedance here of the order of 20,000 ohms (matching a typical transistor output stage) would be:

4 ohms—35:1 ratio
14 ohms—18:1 ratio
60 ohms— 9:1 ratio

Miniature speakers normally have a dc resistance on the order of ohms (nominal 8-ohms impedance), when approximate transformer ratios would be:

30:1 to give an output load impedance of 10,000 ohms
41:1 to give an output load impedance of 20,000 ohms

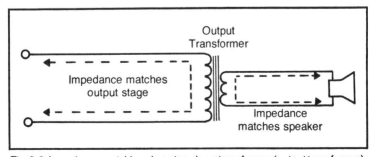

Fig. 8-2. Impedance matching via a step-down transformer (output transformer).

Incidentally, as far as output signal strength is concerned for satisfactory listening, a current of 10 *microamps* represents about the threshold of audibility with high impedance phones. A current of 0.1 *milliamps* is about the minimum level for intelligible listening, and 0.5 *milliamps* the level for comfortable listening. With a current in excess of this value, phones are likely to be swamped and listening becomes uncomfortable. The simple answer in the latter case is to fit a volume control to reduce the signal level if necessary.

Transformer output from a transistor output stage is referred to as Class A operation where the values of the bias and signal voltage applied to the transistor ensure that there is always collector current flowing—Fig. 8-3. This is the simplest type of circuit, but one which is inefficient. Efficiency does not matter so much, for this can be countered by increasing the power of the circuit, but distortion is readily introduced at high listening levels. The main advantage of Class A operation is that it is simple, and quite adequate power can be developed using only a few components.

Generally a more efficient power output can be obtained from a push-pull output stage, using two transistors in the type of circuit shown in Fig. 8-4. This is known as Class B operation. Best performance normally comes from using a complementary pair of transistors (one NPN and one PNP), suitably matched. See Fig. 8-5.

The particular advantage of Class B operation is better quality reproduction with higher efficiency and lower average current drain. The latter can be important in transistor circuits, which are normally battery powered. Class B outputs can, however, generate crossover distortion which is particularly unpleasant to listen to,

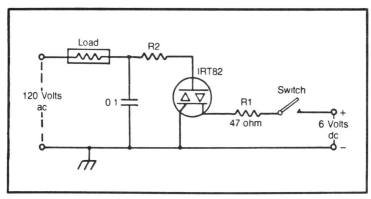

Fig. 8-3. Class A transistor output stage. Component values shown match HEP G0005 or equivalent transistor.

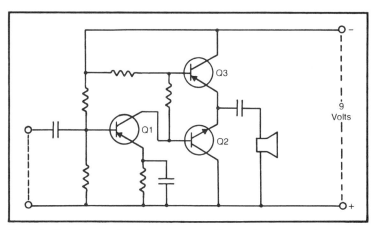

Fig. 8-4. Class B or push-pull output stage with complementary pair (NPN and PNP) output transistors Q2 and Q3.

but which can generally be cured by applying a slight forward bias to each transistor.

The Class B amplifier can also operate as Class AB by arranging that the values of bias and signal voltage applied to each transistor cause collector current to flow appreciably more than half a

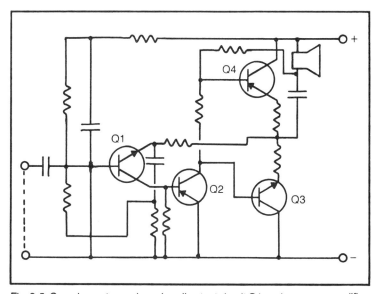

Fig. 8-5. Complementary pair push-pull output circuit Q1 works as a preamplifier. Q2 is the driver for the output push-pull stage Q3 and Q4. Negative feedback is taken from the output to the emitter of Q1.

80

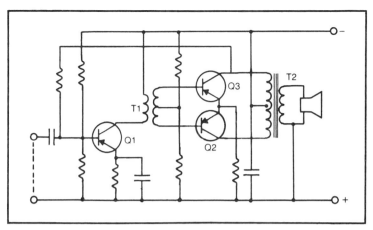

Fig. 8-6. Typical configuration of a push-pull output used in smaller domestic radios. Q1 is the driver with transformer coupling via T1 to the push-pull output stage. T2 is typical transistor output transformer to match impedance loads.

cycle (but always less than a full cycle, otherwise each transistor would be operating in Class A mode). Properly set up, this can result in virtual elimination of distortion.

The basic push-pull output circuit is commonly used with a Class A amplifier as a driver, directly coupled, or transformer coupled. Examples of these two different configurations are shown in Figs. 8-6 and 8-7. In the latter case transformer coupler is also used between the Class B amplifier and the loudspeaker. This is

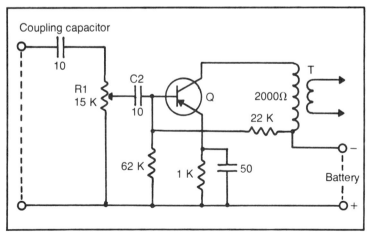

Fig. 8-7. Class B driver circuit. Component values shown match a 2N190 transistor, or equivalent.

virtually the standard type of output used in transistor radios.

Considerably more elaborate treatment is used in hi-fi outputs, where quality and level of distortion is all-important.

CLASS-B DRIVER

This circuit (Fig. 8-7) is virtually a standard form of Class-A amplifier adapted for driving a Class-B output stage via a matching transformer. Circuit components have been kept to a minimum for satisfactory performance. Potentiometer R1 acts both as a potential divider and gain control for the driver, C2 then being necessary to prevent grounding of the base of the transistor.

The output transformer needs to have a primary resistance to match the output impedance required for the transistor used e.g., 2000 ohm for a HEP G0005 transistor, or other types in this group. A 1500 ohm center-tapped secondary provides a suitable input impedance into a typical Class-B amplifier.

Chapter 9

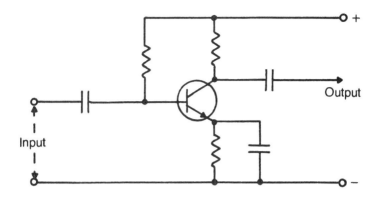

Morse Code Senders

Morse code signals are, traditionally, sent with a key and buzzer. The simple electro-mechanical buzzer has largely been replaced by a transistorized buzzer or simple audio frequency oscillator circuit.

Figure 9-1 shows such a circuit which is very easy to get working. Virtually any general purpose af transistor will do, but the component values shown suit an HEP G0005 or equivalent.

A simple sending key is shown in Fig. 9-2. This comprises a strip of springy brass mounted on a wooden block with two woodscrews. The brass is bent upwards into a cranked shape and a large plastic button glued to the free end with epoxy adhesive to form a knob. Underneath the free end of the spring is a large brass drawing pin or a round-headed brass screw. Key connections are made to this screw and one end of the screws securing the other end of the brass strip. Connect on to one of the battery leads of the buzzer circuit.

To operate, the key should be placed on a table about 18 inches in from the edge. Sit opposite the key, with the right elbow resting near the edge of the table. The knob on the key is *lightly* grasped between finger and thumb and the key operated with a movement of the wrist—not a tapping action. Adjust the spring of the brass strip by further bending, if necessary, to get an easy "sending" action.

To check the working of the circuit, hold the key depressed when a steady tone should be heard in the phones. The volume of this signal can be adjusted by altering the setting of the 50 K

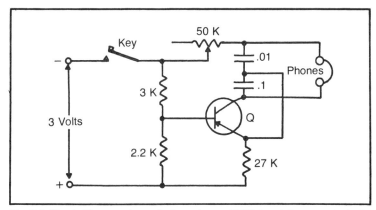

Fig. 9-1. Simple Morse code sender based on an OC71 transistor, or equivalent.

potentiometer. Altering this setting will also tend to change the note of the tone as well, i.e., act as a tone control as well as a volume control. You can also alter the tone of the signal by using different capacitor values. Increasing the value of these capacitors will lower the frequency of the tone; and decreasing the capacitor values will raise the frequency of the tone.

An even simpler "buzzer" circuit is shown in Fig. 9-3 when a 5 K potentiometer replaces the fixed value resistors of the previous circuit. The setting of this is adjusted to get the circuit oscillating (i.e., a tone is heard in the phones). The frequency of this tone will be governed by the values of C1 and C2, in the same manner as before; but for satisfactory working the value of C2 should *always* be ten times greater than C1.

If a volume control is required for this circuit, this takes the

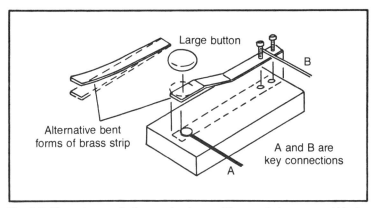

Fig. 9-2. Morse key made from spring brass strip mounted on a wood block.

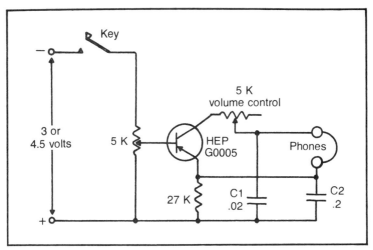

Fig. 9-3. Simplified Morse 'buzzer' circuit.

form of a second 5 K potentiometer connected in the collector lead of the transistor. The key is connected in one of the battery leads, as before.

A more powerful buzzer circuit using an NPN and a PNP transistor is shown in Fig. 9-4. This should have enough power to give a satisfactory tone signal in a small 8-ohm loudspeaker, when powered by a 9-volt battery. The number of components in this

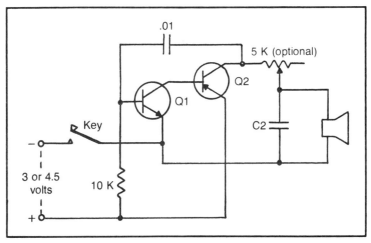

Fig. 9-4. More powerful Morse buzzer circuit. Q1 is an NPN type 2N2102 or equivalent. Q2 is a PNP power transistor type 2N2869 or equivalent. Find best value for C2 by experiment.

circuit have been kept to an absolute minimum, with only one resistor and one capacitor required, apart from the transistors and loudspeaker. If a volume control is required this can be a 2 K or 5 K potentiometer connected in the collector lead of the second transistor (Q2). A tone control could also be added in the form of a variable capacitor connected across the speaker, or try different values of fixed capacitors in this position to give the tone judged most suitable.

Transistor Q1 in this circuit is a NPN type 2N2102, or equivalent. Q2 is a power transistor—type 2N2869, HEP G6013, 40022, or equivalent. This has a metal case with only two leads emerging (marked e for emitter and b for base). The collector lead is connected internally to the case. The collector connection in this circuit is thus made directly to the bolt securing the case to the circuit panel. It is recommended that Q2 be mounted on a heat sink.

Any other type of af oscillator can be used as a Morse code sender, merely by inserting the key in one of the battery supply leads—see chapter on Oscillators.

The Morse Code

A	• ——	di*dah*
B	—— • • •	*dah*dididit
C	—— • —— •	*dah*di*da*dit
D	—— • •	*dah*didit
E	•	dit
F	• • —— •	didi*dah*dit
G	—— —— •	*dahdah*dit
H	• • • •	didididit
I	• •	didit
J	• —— —— ——	di*dahdahdah*
K	—— • ——	dihdi*dah*
L	• —— • •	di*dah*didit
M	—— ——	*dahdah*
N	—— •	*dah*dit
O	—— —— ——	*dahdahdah*
P	• —— —— •	di*dahdah*dit
Q	—— —— • ——	*dahdah*di*dah*
R	• —— •	di*dah*dit
S	• • •	dididit
T	——	*dah*
U	• • ——	didi*dah*
V	• • • ——	dididi*dah*
W	• —— ——	di*dahdah*

X	— • • —	*dah* di di *dah*
Y	— • — —	*dah* di *dahdah*
Z	— — • •	*dahdah* di dit
1	• — — — —	di *dahdahdahdah*
2	• • — — —	di di *dahdahdah*
3	• • • — —	di di di *dahdah*
4	• • • • —	di di di di *dah*
5	• • • • •	di di di di dit
6	— • • • •	*dah* di di di dit
7	— — • • •	*dahdah* di di dit
8	— — — • •	*dahdahdah* di dit
9	— — — — •	*dahdahdahdah* dit
0	— — — — —	*dahdahdahdahdah*

Period	• — • — • —
Comma	— — • • — —
Question mark	• • — — • •
Error	• • • • • • • •
Double dash	— • • • —
Wait	• — • •
End of message	• — • — •
Invitation to transmit	— • —
End of work	• • • — • —

Chapter 10

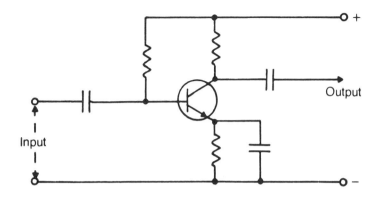

Electronic Organs

A tone generator produces a single note. Depending on the type of circuit involved, it is a simple matter to change the pitch of the note by altering certain component values. If these are arranged in the form of alternative circuits, which can be selected at will, we have the basis of a simple electronic organ capable of playing tunes.

To keep the number of components to a minimum, the starting point can be a Hartley oscillator using a single af transistor of medium power and a transistor output transformer (ignore the center tap). The basic oscillator circuit is shown on the right side of Fig 10-1. This is built on a Paxolin panel allowing enough space at one end to fit eight miniature potentiometers in line. These should be of the carbon preset type, available with either vertical or horizontal mounting, and can be obtained in a diameter size of 1 inch or less. Connections for these types of potentiometers are shown in Fig. 10-2.

In the circuit, two connections only are made to each potentiometer—a common connection to the wiper terminal; and one end of the resistance track of each potentiometer connecting to a separate brass screw mounted on the board. These brass screws are mounted in line and form the keys of the organ.

The common line connects back to the oscillator circuit. The other connection to the circuit is terminated in a probe, e.g., a short length of still plated wire (a spare plug from a meter lead is ideal).

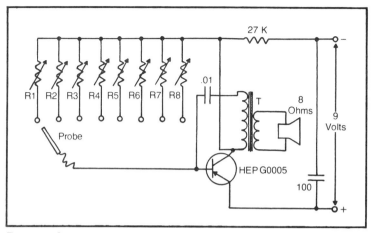

Fig. 10-1. Simple single-transistor electronic organ. The eight potentiometers are all 5K ohm. T is a transistor radio output transformer. All component values as shown on the diagram.

The organ is played by tapping the probe on one of the brass screws at a time. Each will produce a different note heard in the loudspeaker, but first it is necessary to tune the organ.

Starting by holding the probe on one of the middle screws (i.e., R4 or R5), adjust the potentiometer with a screwdriver until the note generated corresponds to middle C of a piano. This can easily be done by ear. Notes are then adjusted on either side, against a piano, until R1 to R8 covers a full octave. Again this is easy to do by

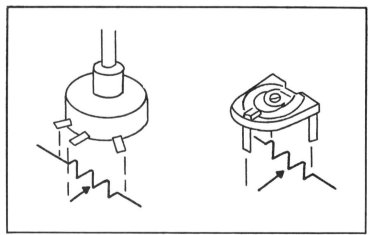

Fig. 10-2. Identifying connections on a standard potentiometer (left) or skeleton, or PC, type (right).

ear—how accurately the organ is tuned depending very much on how musical your ear is!

Once all the potentiometers have been adjusted in this way, you can tap out simple tunes on your electronic organ, note by note. It is also possible to play two notes at once by touching two adjacent screws simultaneously with the probe, although this will "throw" the resultant note well out of the original octave selected and will probably not be all that musical.

If necessary you can also adjust the octave selected up or down by altering the value of the 0.01 μF capacitor. Using a higher value will lower the octave range; using a lower value will raise the octave range. This opens up a further possibility of using two separate capacitors in place of the 0.01 calculator, one giving a treble octave and the other a bass octave. A switch can then be used to switch from one to the other.

There is also the possibility of extending the number of notes to two octaves, i.e., by increasing the number of potentiometers used to fifteen. But this is the limit for this simple circuit.

Another similar electronic organ circuit is shown in Fig. 10-3 based on a Colpitts oscillator. This employs capacitors instead of potentiometers to govern the frequency of the individual tones. No setting-up is required in this case since the fixed value capacitors

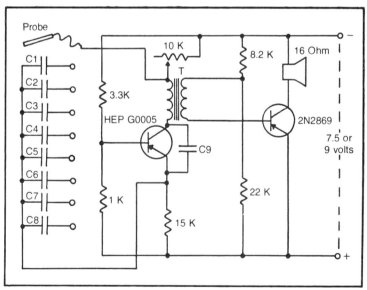

Fig. 10-3. Electronic organ based on a Colpitts oscillator circuit. See text for values of C1 to C8. C1 is 0.01 μF. T is any typical miniature af transformer.

C1 to C8 are selected to give the required resonant frequencies in the circuit with the other component values given. The values to use are:

C1—0.6 μF	C5—0.1 μF
C2—0.33 μF	C6—0.068 μF
C3—0.2 μF	C7—0.05 μF
C4—0.15 μF	C8—0.04 μF

It may be difficult to obtain a complete set of these values and it may be necessary to use mixed capacitor types, e.g., electrolytic and polyester or polycarbonate, etc. If electrolytics or other polarized type(s) are used, it is important to observe the correct polarity of connection into the circuit.

One capacitor lead in each case should again terminate in a brass screw to enable the organ to be played with a probe. There is also the possibility of shifting the octave range by adjusting the value of C9 (a higher value will lower the octave, and vice versa, as before); and using two separate capacitors of different values in place of C9 to switch from one octave to another.

The power developed in this particular circuit is inadequate for loudspeaker operation, although low impedance phones connected directly to the secondary of the transformer would provide adequate listening levels. However, it is a very simple matter to add a single stage of amplification using a power transistor so that the organ can play through a 16-ohm miniature loudspeaker. This amplifier stage is shown on the circuit diagram.

To convert to a "real" electronic organ instead of one where the notes are tapped out by a probe, it is necessary to build a keyboard. This can be quite simple, using strips of springy brass mounted over a contact screw for each switching position, mounted in line as shown in Fig. 10-4. Each strip can then be capped with a fingering key cut from hardwood or balsa strip, glued in place with epoxy adhesive. Connection to the circuit is straightforward. Each contact screw is connected to the individual resistors or capacitors, depending on which circuit is used (taking the place of the row of screws). All keys are then connected correctly and take the place of the probe, i.e., common connection is taken to the transistor base in the oscillator circuit.

The whole keyboard can be built on a suitably substantial base and the electronic circuit mounted underneath, as shown in Fig. 10-5.

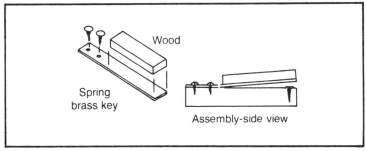

Fig. 10-4. Construction of the individual keys.

A more elaborate organ circuit is shown in Fig. 10-6 which is particularly suitable for keyboard working. The keyboard circuit is shown separately in Fig. 10-6.

This organ differs from the two simple circuits previously described in that it is a multivibrator tone generator rather than an oscillator. It also incorporates a tremolo circuit to enrich the sound, which can be switched in and out. This tremolo circuit, shown in the dashed box on the diagram, is not essential to the working of the organ and can be omitted if desired.

The multivibrator circuit is followed by a single stage of amplification (which must be incorporated), generating enough power to operate an 8 ohm speaker.

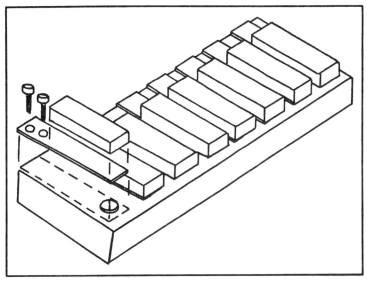

Fig. 10-5. Series of eight keys assembled on a suitable baseboard.

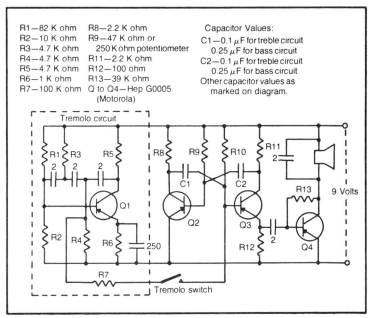

R1—82 K ohm	R8—2.2 K ohm	Capacitor Values:
R2—10 K ohm	R9—47 K ohm or	C1—0.1 μF for treble circuit
R3—4.7 K ohm	250 K ohm potentiometer	0.25 μF for bass circuit
R4—4.7 K ohm	R11—2.2 K ohm	C2—0.1 μF for treble circuit
R5—4.7 K ohm	R12—100 ohm	0.25 μF for bass circuit
R6—1 K ohm	R13—39 K ohm	Other capacitor values as
R7—100 K ohm	Q to Q4—Hep G0005	marked on diagram.
	(Motorola)	

Fig. 10-6. More advanced electronic organ circuit. Additional tremolo circuit shown in dashed box.

The additional keyboard circuit is shown in Fig. 10-7, based on eight 10 K potentiometers. These can be standard miniature, or preset type, depending on the size you intend to make the keyboard. Connection is quite straightforward and each note in the octave is adjusted separately by the setting of its own potentiometer, starting with the end potentiometers associated with key 1.

For a complete electronic organ, two separate keyboards should be made—one for treble and one for base. This will then require two separate electronic circuits to be built complete with its own amplifier and tremolo (if the latter is to be incorporated).

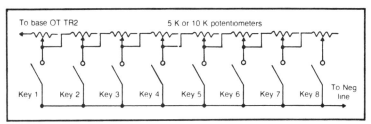

Fig. 10-7. Electronic organ keyboard circuit with potentiometer for individual tone adjustment.

Component values for these two circuits are identical, except for the values of capacitors C5 and C6 as shown in the component list. With a double-banked organ, the treble circuit then connects to (and is initially tuned by) the treble keyboard and its potentiometers. The bass circuit is connected to its own keyboard and tuned one or two more octaves down by its individual potentiometers.

The particular circuit of Fig. 10-6 in fact can be built in six different versions:

1. Simple one-octave organ without tremolo, probe operated.

2. One-octave organ with tremolo, probe operated (the tremolo being switched in or out by switch S1).

3. Simple one-octave organ, without tremolo, keyboard operated.

4. One-octave organ with tremolo, keyboard operated.

5. Treble and bass organ without tremolo, keyboard operated via two keyboards.

6. Treble and bass organ with tremolo, keyboard operated via two keyboards.

Chapter 11

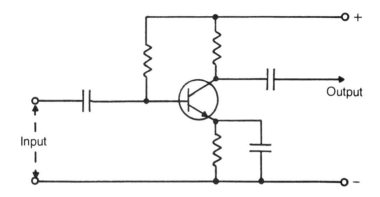

Metal Detectors

A metal detector is basically an audio oscillator which can be upset by the proximity of a metal object. This will cause a marked modification, or even disappearance, of the note heard, with maximum effect when the critical part of the oscillator is nearest to the metal.

This critical component is normally a large diameter coil, which is called the search coil. This is held in a substantially horizontal attitude and passed over the ground or surface beneath which the suspected metal is buried. What happens is that the inductance of the coil (against which the associated circuit is tuned to oscillate) is modified by the presence of adjacent metal, lowering the resonant frequency of the circuit and thus the frequency of oscillation.

As a rough rule the maximum depth to which a search coil will have its inductance sufficiently modified to detect a change in the circuit performance will be equal to the diameter of the coil itself—Fig. 11-1. Thus the larger the diameter of the search coil the better, when searching for buried metal. Unfortunately, however, the larger the physical diameter of the coil the more power is required in the circuit, and the more complicated the circuit needs to be.

A simple low power oscillator circuit can be built around a single inexpensive general-purpose transistor, such as an HEP G0008, associated with a tuned circuit comprising the search coil and a variable capacitor. With suitable proportions for the coil

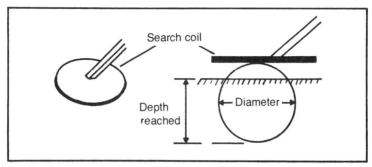

Fig. 11-1. Maximum depth to which a metal detector is sensitive is approximately the same as the search coil diameter.

will have a frequency of oscillator of, perhaps, 100 to 500 kHz in a Hartley circuit, the actual oscillating frequency being determined by the setting of the variable capacitor. This is well above audio frequency range, but a simple oscillator circuit of this type will have a low frequency component which will be made audible by rectification. This function can be performed by a diode. This type of af/rf oscillator is known as a beat-frequency oscillator.

A complete circuit of this type is shown in Fig. 11-2. L1 is the search coil which, in combination with variable capacitor C2, forms the resonant circuit. D1 is a germanium diode that rectifies the rf oscillation and feeds a dc component signal of the audio frequency content to the phones. L2 is a radio frequency choke with an induction of about 2 or 3 millihenries. This and all the other components can be bought as standard items, except for the search coil (L1) which must be specially wound.

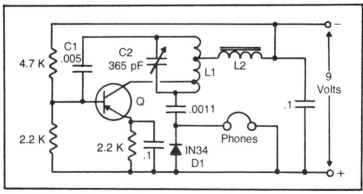

Fig. 11-2. Simple low-power (low diameter search coil) metal detector. L1 is the search coil, L2 a 2 or 3 millihenry RFC choke. Other component values as marked on diagram.

98

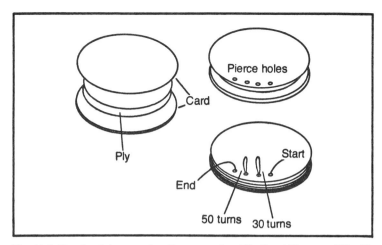

Fig. 11-3. Details of the search coil construction. Winding 100 turns of No. 28 enamelled wire.

For the power developed in this circuit a suitable size of search coil is 6 inches diameter. A suitable former of this size can be cut from ¼-inch plywood, which is then capped in either side with 6 ½-inch diameter circles of stiff card—Fig. 11-3. Pierce four small holes in one of the card discs, as shown, through which the coil winding wire is taken for connections.

The coil itself consists of 100 turns of #28 enameled wire, tapped at 30 turns and 50 turns. In other word, just pass the end of the wire through the start hole, wind on 30 turns and take a loop through the next hole. Wind another 20 turns and take another loop

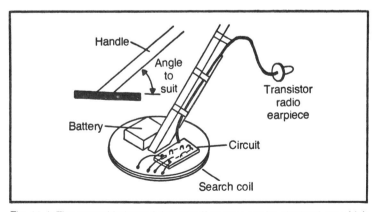

Fig. 11-4. The assembled metal detector. If no tone can be obtained, try a high impedance deaf-aid earpiece instead of a transistor radio earpiece.

through the third hole. Then wind on another 50 turns and take the end through the last hole. Secure the winding in place with a wrapping of insulating tape.

The actual circuit is assembled on a perf board. When completed, this board can be mounted on top of the search coil former and the four search coil connections made to the circuit, as indicated. The 9-volt battery can be mounted on the other side of the search coil former to balance (e.g., in clips or a simple box). The addition of a handle then completes the assembly—Fig. 11-4.

An on-off switch can be mounted on the handle (in one of the battery leads). Phone connections are taken up the handle and taped in position to secure. Leave enough length of lead to connect to the phones, with adequate slack to maneuver the search coil at ground level while wearing the phones.

Any high impedance phones should be suitable for this circuit but since the device is a miniaturized one it is recommended that a high impedance earpiece be used rather than hi-fi type earphones.

To check the circuit for working, switch on and adjust the variable capacitor C2 until a steady note is heard in the earpiece (it may be necessary to add more, fixed, capacitance in parallel with C1). Now bring the search coil over a metal object, e.g., a coin. The note heard should drop in frequency, or disappear completely. If the change note is not very marked, try adjusting the variable capacitor to a different note and repeat the test. If the result is better, further adjust C2 in the same direction until the note disappears when the search coil is over metal. If results are worse, adjust C2 in the opposite direction until optimum response is obtained.

You may also be able to improve the performance of your simple metal detector by increasing the number of turns on the search coil, e.g., adding additional turns at each end.

A more powerful metal detector circuit is shown in Fig. 11-5, incorporating both a search coil and a local oscillation coil. The latter is inductively tuned, implying that it is wound on a core and that core is adjusted until a beat note is heard in the phones. The variable capacitor in this case is merely for adjustment. The rf signal extracted from this circuit is again rectified by a diode, but this is followed by two stages of amplification.

The search coil in this case can be made very much larger, e.g., 18 or 20 inches in diameter. Because of this increased diameter a much smaller number of turns is required. Recommended windings (again for wire) is 15 complete turns, tapped at 5 turns, 6 turns and 10 turns.

100

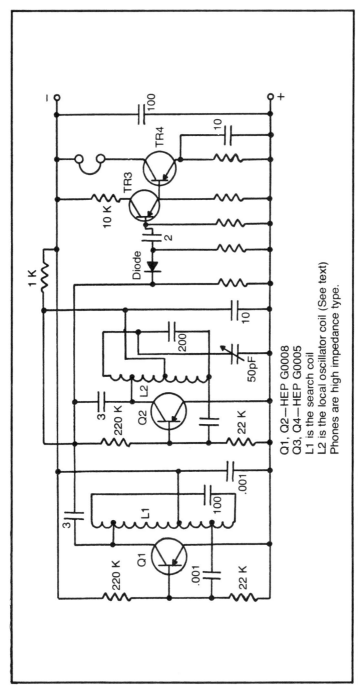

Fig. 11-5. Circuit for a more powerful metal detector using a search coil of 18 or 20 inch diameter. Component values as shown.

Q1, Q2—HEP G0008
Q3, Q4—HEP G0005
L1 is the search coil
L2 is the local oscillator coil (See text)
Phones are high impedance type.

101

All the other components are standard, except for the local oscillation coil L2. This consists of 120 turns of #38 enameled wire wound on a ⅜-inch diameter former, tapped at 20 turns and 40 turns. It is important to get these tapping points connected the right way round in the circuit. Other component values are as specified in the parts list.

Final assembly of the metal detector can be similar to Fig. 11-4, with the search coil wound on a ply former; circuit panel mounted on top, with battery on the other side to balance. A stouter handle is required to carry the additional weight of the large diameter coil former and will need bracing to the ply.

To set up the detector, switch on and adjust the dust core of L2 until a satisfactory note is heard. Bring the search coil over some metal object, when the note should fade appreciably. Holding this position, adjust the 50 pF variable capacitor until the note disappears entirely. The circuit is then set up for optimum performance.

If unable to obtain satisfactory results, remove one turn from *each* end of the search coil winding and try again. If good results are still difficult to obtain, you could try changing transistors Q1 and Q2 for higher gain types.

Chapter 12

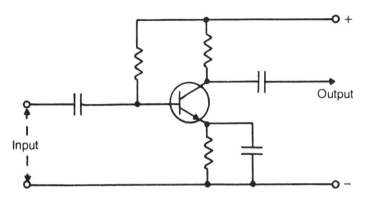

Multivibrators and Flip-Flops

A *multivibrator* is another form of oscillating circuit which automatically switches from one conducting state to another, and back again, and so on. This is also known as a flip-flop. Oscillation can occur at high frequency, and so such a circuit can be used as an audio tone generator. Equally, however, a multivibrator can be adjusted to oscillate at a very low frequency—one or two cycles per second or even slower. This can be used as a working circuit for clock or timing devices, like the *metronome*.

A basic flip-flop (multivibrator) circuit consists of two cross-linked transistors, working in an unstable state, as shown in Fig. 12-1. Slight unbalance in the component values, or anything else that contributes to random variations in current will cause one transistor to switch off, switching the other on. The on transistor will then switch off, switching the other on . . . and so on.

The frequency at which this will occur depends on the transistor characteristics and the associated component values. For example, in the circuit shown, using HEP G0005 transistors (or equivalents), the following component values will give an oscillation frequency of about 5 kHz:

> R1— 1 K
> R2—27 K
> R3—27 K
> R4— 1 K
> C1 and C2—4700 pF

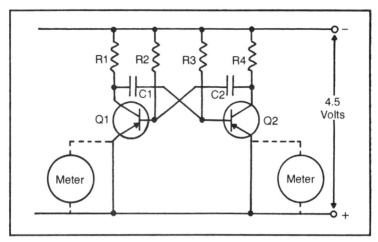

Fig. 12-1. Basic circuit for a multivibrator. Resistor values depend on transistors used: these and capacitors C1 and C2 govern frequency of oscillation (see text).

Using the same transistors the frequency of oscillation can be reduced to about 1 Hz or 2 Hz (once or twice per second):

R1—10 K
R2—10 K
R3— 1 K
R4— 1 K
C1 and C2—100 μF

The higher frequency working could be listened to, as a tone, by replacing R4 with a high impedance earpiece. The low frequency working could not be heard in this manner but could be indicated by connecting two 0.5 volt voltmeters to the circuit, as shown dotted.

Exactly the same circuit can be used to make a flasher. In this case, using the transistors originally specified there will be insufficient power to operate a light bulb and so an additional amplifier (Q2) is needed. This can be an HEP G6003 or similar transistor, connected to one end of the circuit as shown in Fig. 12-2 with a 3.5-volt flashlight bulb in the emitter lead. This bulb will flash on and off at the same rate as the multivibrator frequency. Remember the actual flashing frequency can be adjusted by experimenting with different values of E1, R2, R3 and R4, and the two capacitors (which should always be of the same value). First try adding a 100 K potentiometer in series with R3 if you want to experiment. Do not replace R3 directly with the potentiometer. Leaving this resistance

104

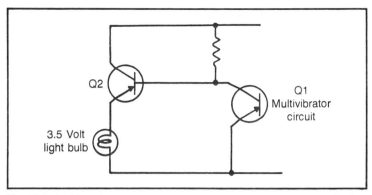

Fig. 12-2. Addition of transistor amplifier to basic multivibrator circuit to 'flash' a 3.5-volt flashlight bulb.

in circuit protects the transistors against accidental overload.

By adjusting the flashing rate very carefully against a stopwatch, you should be able to aim at a setting giving exactly one flash per second. Then you have a flashing clock, each tick or second being indicated by the bulb flashing once. This makes a useful form of timer for operations requiring seconds to be counted accurately. Enclose the bulb in a safelight color screen and you have a useful enlarger timer.

An identical flasher circuit (HEP G6003 transistor and bulb) can, of course, also be connected to the other end of the circuit. One bulb will then flash on as the other switches off.

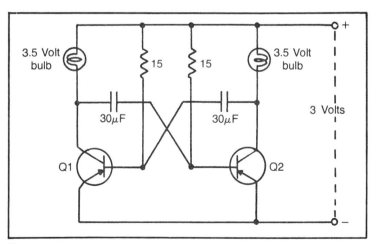

Fig. 12-3. Compact "flasher" circuit based on two 2N1304 or HEP G0011 transistors.

Using higher power transistors the flasher can be made to work without the necessity of an additional amplifying transistor for each bulb. The bulb can also be used to replace one (or both) bias resistors. The flasher circuit then reduces to that shown in Fig. 12-3. A simple circuit of this type, built down to the smallest possible size, could work realistic winking lights on a model airplane.

METRONOME

The same basic multivibrator circuit of Fig. 12-1 using HEP G0005 transistors (or equivalent) can be connected to a 4-ohm loudspeaker to provide an audible output or beat note at the oscillating frequency ranging from about one every three seconds to three times a second. This covers the usual range required for a metronome. The complete circuit is shown in Fig. 12-4 with matched component values given in the schematic. The 250 K potentiometer is a frequency control. Adjusting this will vary the note of "beating" heard in the loudspeaker. A 10 K resistor in series with the potentiometer is advisable to limit the maximum current flowing in this in the event of the potentiometer being turned to zero resistance.

This same metronome circuit can be extended to operate a flashing lamp (or series of lamps) simultaneously with the audible note in the loudspeaker. For optimum results the two transistors used in the multivibrator circuit should be closely matched in characteristics. An HEP G6003 (or equivalent) transistor will

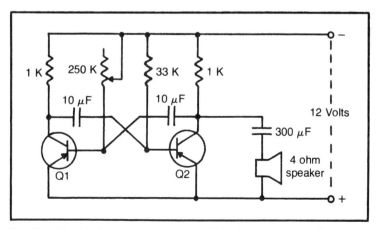

Fig. 12-4. Variable frequency metronome with loud speaker output. Power by a 12-volt battery.

106

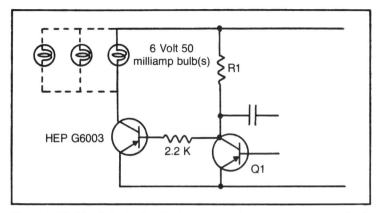

Fig. 12-5. Flashing light circuit added to one end of the basic metronome circuit. Q1 and R1 are components of the metronome circuit.

supply the necessary power amplification for the lamp(s), connected as shown in Fig. 12-5. Here two alternatives are shown—a single lamp circuit, or a series of lamps connected in parallel. Up to four lamps can be operated simultaneously. The HEP G6003 will power a large number of lamps, if required, but in this case should be mounted on a heat sink to dissipate the self-heating from the higher current passed.

A metronome can also be built around a *single* unijunction transistor which has inherently unstable or oscillating characteristics. Such a circuit is shown in Fig. 12-6. This is a relaxation

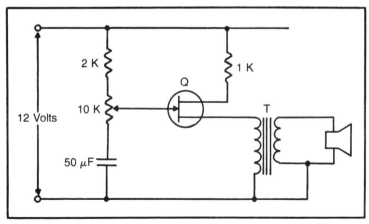

Fig. 12-6. Single transistor metronome based on a unijunction transistor, 2N2646 or equivalent. Component values are shown on the diagram. The transformer (T) is a typical output transformer for, or from, a transistor radio.

107

oscillator and not a true multivibrator circuit, although it provides the same end result, i.e., an adjustable beat note heard in the loudspeaker. Beat note is adjustable via the potentiometer in the emitter (or gate) circuit.

The transformer used is a transistor output transformer with primary center tap. The circuit may not work with the transistor connected across the full primary, in which case connect to the center tap. Virtually any unijunction type transistor should work in this circuit, using the component values given in the caption. If necessary a tone and/or volume control can be added in the output circuit from the transformer secondary to the loudspeaker. For volume control, connect a 1 K or 5 K potentiometer in one of the leads to the speaker. To combine with a tone control, connect a 1 μF capacitor across the speaker terminals. Experiment with different capacitor values for best effect.

Chapter 13

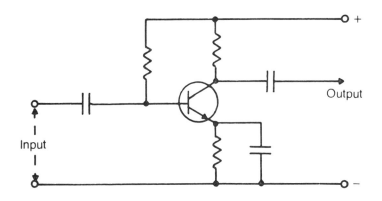

Light-Operated Devices

Light sensitive devices fall into two main categories:

1. Those which are activated when illuminated by a light source such as daylight. These include *photoelectric* cells and solar batteries, either of which can be used as a source of power in electronic circuits.

2. Components which change their electrical resistance characteristics when light falls on them. These include *photodiodes* which have no-go, go characteristics (work like a switch); *light-activated silicon controlled rectifiers* (LASCRx), which have a similar switching action to photo-diodes; and *phototransistors* which combine a switching action with amplification.

Figure 13-1 shows a simple switching, circuit based on a photo transistor. The transistor acts as a variable resistance device. Light falling on it decreases its resistance and this increases the current flowing through the emitter-collector circuit causing the relay to pull in. As the level of light falls off the resistance in this circuit decreases, until a point is reached when the relay drops out.

A suitable relay coil resistance to match phototransistor is 3000-5000 ohms. The relay should be of the sensitive type capable of being adjusted to pull-in at a current of about 2 milliamps. The potentiometer is included in the circuit to provide final adjustment of the circuit to available light (and to different relay coil resistances).

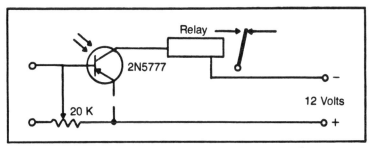

Fig. 13-1. Simple switching circuit based on a phototransistor. The relay contacts provide the switch action for an external circuit.

The relay contacts are connected to an external alarm circuit. Connected as shown in Fig. 13-2A, the bulb lights, or the buzzer sounds, when the relay is pulled in. When the light level falls the bulb goes out (or the buzzer stops). Current to the other relay contact as in Fig. 13-2B, the bulb lights up, or the buzzer sounds, only when the light level falls below a predetermined level (as originally adjusted by the potentiometer).

Instead of a bulb or buzzer the relay contacts could equally well be used to switch an electronic circuit on and off, e.g., a simple af oscillator circuit.

An improved version of this circuit is shown in Fig. 13-3 where a second (ordinary) transistor is added to provide further amplification. This is a much more sensitive circuit, i.e., will respond or "switch" at much smaller changes in the level of illumination of the phototransistor. The circuit is set up for working as follows:

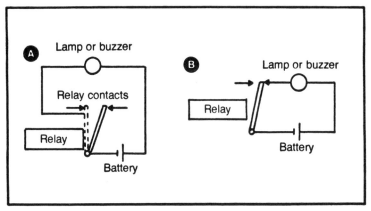

Fig. 13-2A. Switches on lamp or buzzer when relay is pulled in. B Operates lamp or buzzer when light level falls.

110

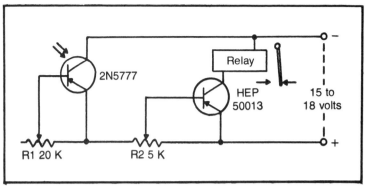

Fig. 13-3. Photoelectric switching circuit with improved sensitivity.

1. Adjust the relay to pull-in at a current of about 2 milliamps.

2. With the phototransistor completely shielded from light (e.g., covered over) adjust R2 so that the relay drops out with the circuit switched on. Check by switching off and on again that the relay does not pull in when switched on.

3. Adjust R1 with the phototransistor uncovered so that the relay pulls in at the level of illumination required.

For greater sensitivity readjust R2 to be nearer the relay pull-in point; and then readjust R1 as necessary. Again the relay contacts can be used to switch an af oscillator circuit instead of a bulb or buzzer alarm circuit.

A disadvantage of both these circuits is that there is a steady current drain in the battery all the while the circuit is switched on. This can be reduced to a minimum by using a slightly different circuit employing a *photocell* instead of a phototransistor. An ordinary transistor is then used as an amplifier.

The complete circuit is shown in Fig. 13-4. Relay resistance can be anything up to 5 K. Potentiometer R2 provides a means of adjusting the current flowing to match the coil resistance of the relay used. The relay should be adjusted to pull-in at about 2 milliamps or less.

The 500 K potentiometer is a sensitivity control for the circuit, i.e., sets the circuit to work at the level of illumination required. It can also be used to set the current drain to an absolute minimum level when the photocell is not illuminated, increasing the life of the battery when the circuit is to be left switched on for a long time (e.g., for use as an alarm). The more this potentiometer can be adjusted to leave as much resistance in circuit as possible the better. (Check for

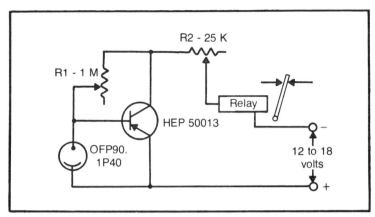

Fig. 13-4. Photoelectric switching circuit based on an old style photoelectric cell suitable for relays with coil resistances up to 5 K ohms.

minimum current flow with a milliammeter inserted in one of the battery leads.) At the same time it must not leave too much resistance in circuit, otherwise when the photocell is illuminated the current rise may not be enough for the relay to pull in. The use of a sensitive relay which can be adjusted to a low pull-in current is therefore an advantage.

Again the sensitivity of such a circuit can be improved enormously by adding an additional stage of amplification, as shown in Fig. 13-5. Also in this case the current when the relay is not operated is virtually negligible, rising to 5 milliamps or more when

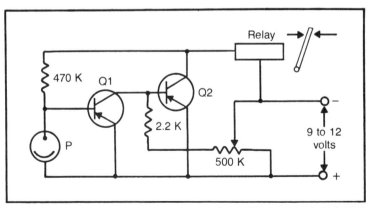

Fig. 13-5. Amplified photocell switching circuit. P is OFP90 photocell. Q1 is HEP G0005 or equivalent. Q2 is HEP G6006 or equivalent. The 500 K potentiometer acts as an overall sensitivity control. A 1 Meg potentiometer can be substituted for the 470 K ohm resistor.

the photocell is illuminated.

Two controls are available for setting up. The 500 K potentiometer controls the overall sensitivity of the circuit. If a 1 Meg potentiometer is substituted for the 470 K resistor, this provides a means of varying the *switching time* of the circuit, or the time delay occurring between pull-in and drop-out of the relay.

Photoswitch circuits like these have a wide application as burglar alarms as well as counter circuits, etc., responding to interruption of a light beam directed at the light-sensitive element (photocell or phototransistor)—apart from their obvious use as warnings of when the level of daylight, or other illumination, rises above, or falls below, a certain level. In this latter form of application, such a circuit could be used to switch on artificial lighting when the daylight falls to a certain level. If a mains circuit is to be switched, however, this should be done through a second heavy-duty "slave" relay with mains-rated contacts capable of carrying the necessary load. The light switch relay then simply closes the circuit for the slave relay, as shown in Fig. 13-6.

Such a precaution is not necessary when the artificial lighting is a low voltage bulb. This can, in fact, be switched directly with an all-transistor circuit using a power transistor for the final stage of amplification, eliminating the need for a relay at all. Such a circuit is shown in Fig. 13-7.

This is basically the same type of photocell circuit followed by two stages of current amplification via Q1 and Q2. Component values shown are for use with a 6-volt battery and 6 volt 3-watt bulb. To use the same circuit for a parking light, which automatically

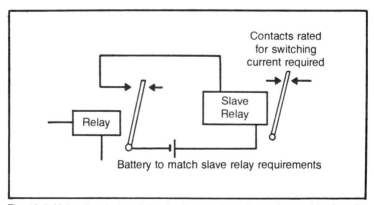

Fig. 13-6. Using the photoswitch relay to operate a slave relay enables heavier currents to be switched by the slave relay contacts.

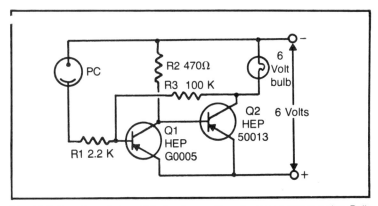

Fig. 13-7. Relayless photoswitch circuit operating a lamp as a signal device. Bulb lights when light level falls. Substitute a 5K potentiometer for the 2.2K resistor for a sensitivity control.

switches on when the daylight falls, connect to a 12-volt car battery and use 12 volt lamps. Component values needed are:

R1—10 K
R2—1000 K
R3—220 K

In this case the bulb should be a 12 volt 2 watt or 12 volt 3 watt type.

Fitted to a car, the photocell should be in a place exposed to maximum illumination, e.g., one corner of a windshield or rear window (the whole circuit can be mounted in this position, or just the photocell). The lamp is separate from the circuit, housed in a "parking light" fitting on the outside of the car. Battery connecting leads are taken to the car battery and a suitable car ground point, respectively. The battery lead should incorporate a 1-amp fuse.

MODULATED LIGHT SWITCH

All the circuits so far described work on steady levels of illumination, e.g., daylight or light from a battery-powered bulb. It is also possible to make a light switch respond only to "pulsation" or modulated light sources. This has the advantage of making the device free from interference from stray light sources and respond only to its particular modulated light source (e.g., a lamp working from an ac source).

A modulated light switch circuit is shown in Fig. 13-8 together with the necessary component values. The 100 K ohm potentiome-

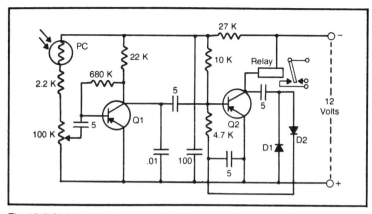

Fig. 13-8. Light switch alarm circuit which works off modulated light. Q1 and Q2 are HEP G0005 or equivalent transistors. D1 and D2 are germanium diodes such as 1N34.

ter is the sensitivity control. It should be possible to use virtually any sensitive relay in this circuit having coil resistance between 1 K and 10 K.

ALARM CIRCUIT WITH "RESET"

Figure 13-9 shows a very simple light switch circuit using a two pole relay with a coil resistance of 2 K or 3 K and a photocell. Provided the relay can be adjusted to pull in at a current of 3 to 4 milliamps, no difficulty should be experienced in getting this circuit

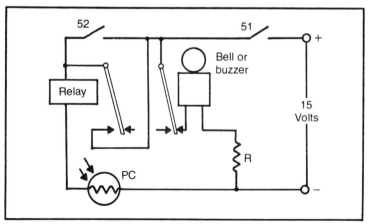

Fig. 13-9. Light switch circuit with reset. The value of resistor R is found by experiment to suit the resistance of the bell or buzzer coils. Switch S2 for reset action. PC is a cadmium sulfide photocell available from hobbyist part sources.

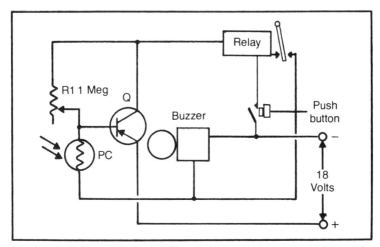

Fig. 13-10. Light switch circuit with self-holding facilities. Circuit is reset by pushbutton switch PBS. Transistor type used is HEP S0013 or equivalent.

to work, adjusting the value of resistor R to suit the resistance of the bell or buzzer used.

Switch S1 switches on the circuit, when the buzzer or bell will sound. With the photocell illuminated, momentary depression of the push-button switch S2 will cause the relay to pull in, switching off the bell or buzzer. The circuit will then remain in this state until the light beam to the photocell is interrupted. Immediately after this happens the relay will drop out causing the bell or buzzer to operate. It will continue sounding an alarm even if the light source is restored.

In other words, the alarm is triggered by a momentary interruption of the light to the photocell. Pressing switch S2 will then reset the circuit to its original state. This is a more effective form of burglar alarm than one which only sounds a warning during the period the light beam is interrupted.

Another trigger alarm circuit with reset is shown in Fig. 13-10, this time requiring only a relay with a single set of changeover contacts.

Adjust the potentiometer R1 until the relay just drops out with the photocell illuminated. Any interruption of the light should then cause the relay to pull in and hold in (completing the alarm circuit through its contacts) even when illumination is restored. The push-button is a press-to-break type and is the reset switch. Operating it causes the relay to drop out and "reset" the alarm circuit.

Chapter 14

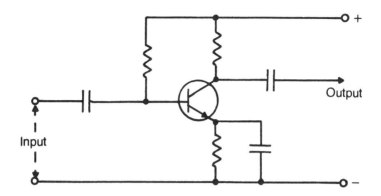

Light-Beam Radio

Sound may be transmitted by light beams as well as radio waves. For such a method of working a transmitter is required which converts sound input through a microphone into a varying current which is then used to modulate the light output given by a bulb in the circuit. This sound-modulated light is then beamed to a receiver, the detector part of which is a photodiode or phototransistor. Output from this detector is in the form of a dc current modulated at the same frequency as the beam. The rest of the receiver circuit extracts and amplifies this af component so that it can be heard in phones or a loudspeaker, depending on the amount of amplification employed.

A circuit for a light-beam transmitter is shown in Fig. 14-1. This comprises a crystal microphone followed by a high-gain amplifier. The output of the amplifier feeds a 2.5- or 3.5-volt flashlight bulb. With the circuit switched on, the 10 K potentiometer is adjusted until the bulb glows brightly, but not at full intensity, which could result in it burning out in a short time.

Speaking into the microphone should then modulate the light emitted by the bulb, i.e., cause the light to vary in intensity at the same frequency as the speech waves. It should be possible to observe this effect if the transmitter is tried out in a darkened room. This will confirm that the transmitter is "working."

The receiver circuit can be kept very simple for a start. Using an International Rectifier S1M, or equivalent, photocell as a de-

117

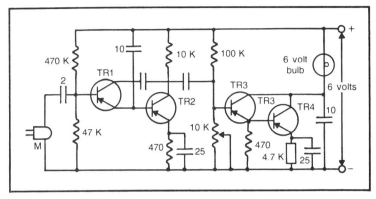

Fig. 14-1. Circuit for a light-beam transmitter. Component values are as shown. TR1, TR2, and TR3 are OC72 transistors, or equivalent. M is a crystal microphone.

tector this can be coupled directly to a conjunction transistor via a 1:10 transformer, as shown in Fig. 14-2. The 1 megohm potentiometer provides the necessary bias and also acts as a volume control. R2 and C2 provide stabilization of the transistor, but can be omitted. The transformer is a typical transistor output transformer used the other way around, i.e., output side connected to the photo transistor and "input" side to the transistor. High impedance headphones (rather than a single earpiece) should be used.

The weakest link in the system is the light-beam path. The transmitter bulb should be mounted in a good reflector, adjusting the bulb position carefully to give a concentrated parallel beam. A flashlight reflector can be used but one taken from a car spotlight would probably be better.

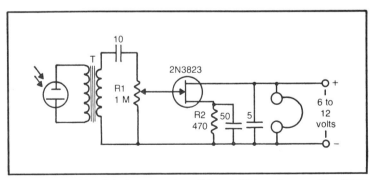

Fig. 14-2. Matching light-beam receiver. T is a 1:10 transformer with primary resistance 200 ohms and secondary resistance 2000 ohms or a 10:1 transformer connected the opposite way around (Argonne AR-123).

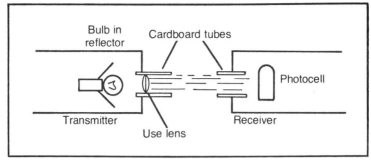

Fig. 14-3. Ideally a light-beam transmitter should direct a parallel beam of light directly into the receiver photocell. Phones are high-impedance type.

The whole of the receiver should be enclosed in a light-tight box with an opening immediately opposite the photo transistor. The photo transistor must be positioned so that the light-sensitive side is facing towards this opening. A small card or plastic tube should be fitted into the opening to assist in focusing the transmitter light beam on the receiver detector—see Fig. 14-3. Obviously, too, the transmitter must be positioned so as to direct its light beam directly onto the receiver tube.

The effective range over which satisfactory transmission can be achieved can prove relatively short. That is why headphones are preferred to an earpiece for listening. They blank off direct reception of sound. Nevertheless this form of speech transmission is

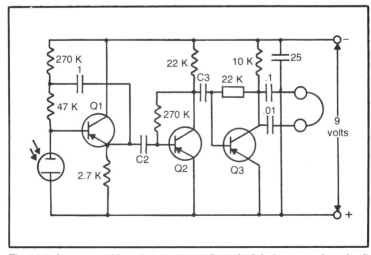

Fig. 14-4. A more sensitive—but more complicated—light-beam receiver circuit Q1, Q2, Q3 and HEPG0005 transistors, or equivalent.

119

sufficiently different and technically interesting to justify trying out, even if only on an experimental basis.

It is possible to improve the range by building a more sensitive receiver, i.e., incorporating a greater degree of light input signal amplification. It also helps particularly to amplify the higher frequencies in the modulated signal, since these are somewhat highly attenuated by a light-beam transmitter. A circuit of this type is shown in Fig. 14-4 where it is recommended that the optimum values of C2 and C3 be found by trial and error, using the *lowest* values which give satisfactory results.

Chapter 15

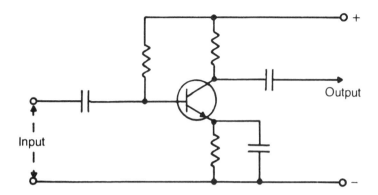

Temperature-Sensitive Devices

Thermistors are temperature-sensitive resistors, the actual resistance offered by the device in a circuit depending on its temperature. As a thermistor gets hotter its resistance decreases, and vice versa. Connected in a simple circuit, together with a meter, a thermistor can be used to measure temperature.

The basic circuit for an electronic thermometer is shown in Fig. 15-1. Battery voltage and milliammeter range are selected to match the resistance characteristics of the thermistor available. Battery voltage must be such that, for a given minimum thermistor resistance (hot resistance), the current flowing through the circuit must not exceed the maximum rating for the meter, i.e., max. battery voltage = max. meter current × min. thermistor resistance. Thus, for a 50 milliamp meter

$$\text{max. battery voltage} = \frac{\text{min. thermistor resistance}}{20}$$

For example, the measuring temperature range required is, say, up to 150° F and the quoted thermistor resistance at this temperature is 60 ohms:

$$\text{max. battery voltage} = \frac{60}{20} = 3 \text{ volts}$$

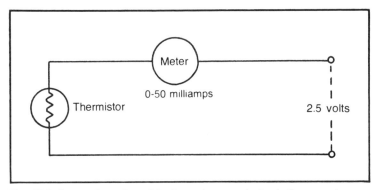

Fig. 15-1. Connecting a thermistor to work as an electronic thermometer.

This means that if the milliammeter reads 50 the temperature indicated is 150° F. The milliamp scale can be calibrated directly in degrees temperature by comparison with a standard thermometer at different temperatures, or calculated from the full resistance / temperature characteristics of the thermistor, if known.

Such a simple circuit has distinct limitations in sensitivity and accuracy of reading. An electronic thermometer will perform better if the thermistor circuit is amplified and read by a more sensitive (i.e., lower working range) milliammeter, as shown in Fig. 15-2. The potentiometer included enables the circuit to be adjusted for maximum meter reading at minimum thermistor resistance, ensuring that the full range of the meter is used for readings. The

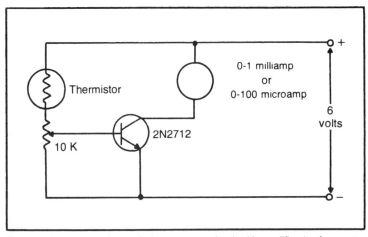

Fig. 15-2. Thermistor electronic thermometer circuit with amplification for greater sensitivity.

milliammeter scale can only be calculated in terms of equivalent temperatures by direct comparison with another thermometer at different temperatures. Note, however, that in both circuits described, zero temperature will always occur at some positive-scale reading on the meter.

A particular attraction of the simple electronic thermometer is that the temperature-sensing device (the thermistor) can be quite remote from the indicating device (the meter). Thus the thermistor can be outdoors for measuring outside temperatures, coupled by two thin insulated wires to the meter circuit indoors.

Chapter 16

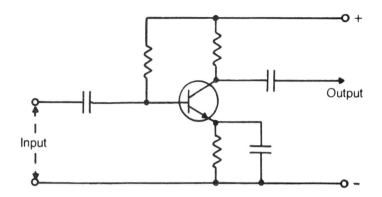

Inductive-Loop Radio Control

Inductive-loop radio control needs a preliminary explanation for most modelers are unfamiliar with the system. It is essentially a short-range control system, the field covered by the control being limited by a large circle, square, or rectangle or wire forming the "inductive loop." That more or less limits it to simple radio control applications of devices or models which only move slowly and can be controlled within a restricted space (e.g., a model car or land vehicle).

The control loop is provided by a transmitter and receiver in the usual way, the receiver being connected to a suitable actuator for controlling the model or device concerned. The only real advantage of an inductive-loop system is that relatively simple circuits are required for the transmitter and receiver. There is also the fact that the system is virtually interference free within the loop although it could be affected by other electrical devices working within the loop. Similarly, the system will not interfere with other electrical appliances, etc., unless this is also located inside the loop, or close to the wire forming the loop.

THE TRANSMITTER

Figure 16-1 shows a suitable circuit for the transmitter. This is an oscillator circuit with amplification and employes four transistors. Amplifier stages and output are transformer coupled. A fairly large number of components are involved but this is necessary to

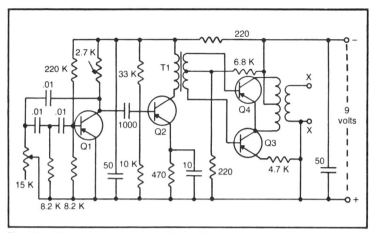

Fig. 16-1. Transmitter circuit for inductive-loop radio control. T1 is a 5:1 transformer. T2 is a 10:1 transformer. Inductive loop (see Fig. 16-2) connects to output of T2 at X-X. Key signal by switch in battery lead. The transistors are HEP G0005, or equivalent.

enough output power. The circuit is, however, quite straightforward to construct and can be built into compact form on a perfboard.

Power is supplied by a 9-volt battery. The switch in one battery lead should be a push-button type, or better still a microswitch. As well as acting as an on-off switch for the transmitter, this

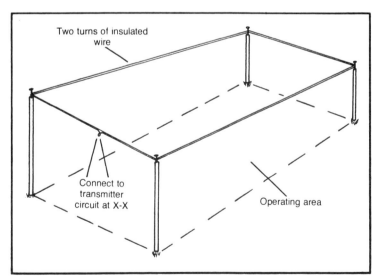

Fig. 16-2. The inductive loop is a winding of thin enameled wire taken around posts. Area enclosed by loop receives the transmitter signal.

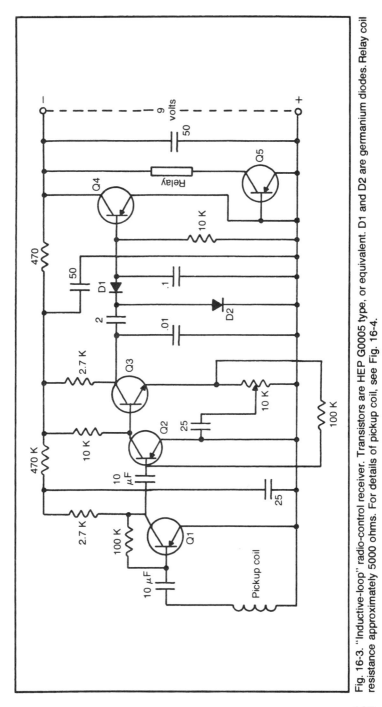

Fig. 16-3. "Inductive-loop" radio-control receiver. Transistors are HEP G0005 type, or equivalent. D1 and D2 are germanium diodes. Relay coil resistance approximately 5000 ohms. For details of pickup coil, see Fig. 16-4.

127

also forms the keying switch by means of which transmitter signals are sent.

THE INDUCTIVE LOOP

This is two turns of any thin, insulated wire encircling the area over which control is required, e.g., taken around the walls of a room. Outdoors it could be strung between poles about 3 feet high—Fig. 16-2. Maximum size to suit the transmitter would be "legs" about 15 feet long (or a circle of about 15 feet diameter). Inside a room, simply use the full dimensions of the room.

THE RECEIVER

The receiver circuit is shown in Fig. 16-3. It uses rather more components than the transmitter, but again is quite straightforward to construct and can be built in a compact size using subminiature resistors and capacitors. All are standard radio components except for the pickup coil and relay.

The pickup coil replaces the antenna and tuned circuit on a conventional radio receiver. It consists of a single winding of 3000 turns of #40 enameled wire on a ⅜-inch diameter ferrite rod—see Fig. 16-4. Fit the rod with ¾-inch diameter cheeks cut from stiff card spaced 1 inch apart and wind the coil layer-on-layer. For rapid winding, bind one end of the ferrite rod with insulating tape and grip in the jaws of a hand drill. Mount the drill horizontally in a vise and use a mechanical winder to reel on the 3000 turns required. When the winding is complete, bind with insulating tape to hold in place.

The relay should have a coil resistance of approximately 2000 ohms. Any sensitive or high-speed relay should do, but preferably use one specially made for radio-control receivers. These may be hard to find since most modern radio-control receivers are now

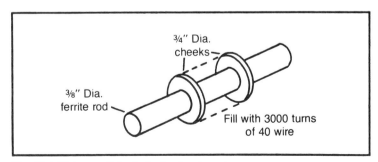

Fig. 16-4. Pick-up coil for 'inductive loop' receiver.

relayless and there is less demand for relays, but a shop specializing in radio-control equipment for models should be able to provide one.

Some adjustment of the relay may be necessary to get it to pull-in and drop-out under the influence of the transmitter being keyed on and off, respectively. As an initial check, connect a 500 milliamp meter in one of the receiver leads and observe the current change when the transmitter is keyed on and off. Adjust the potentiometer for maximum current change. If the relay does not respond to this current change, then adjust it until it does.

The relay works as an on-off switch to control the actuator. This can be an electromagnetic type (e.g., an escapement) or motorized type (e.g., an electric motor or single-channel motorized actuator).

Chapter 17

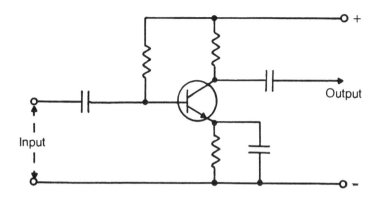

More Instruments

Testing or measuring sometimes calls for measuring very low currents of the order of microamps. Microammeters are relatively expensive instruments and far less rugged than readily obtainable milliammeters. However, it is easy to convert a milliammeter into a microammeter by fitting a dc amplifier circuit to the meter. The only practical disadvantage of such circuits is that they have a high input resistance, resulting in an appreciable voltage drop. They cannot, therefore, be used for microamp measurements in circuits where voltage drop can appreciably affect the accuracy of reading required.

Figure 17-1 shows a microammeter circuit based around a 0-1 milliamp meter and a general purpose PNP transistor HEP G0005 or equivalent. Potentiometer R4 is the zero set adjustment, used to set the meter reading to zero with no EC input to the circuit. R3 is the calibration control used to adjust the meter to full scale when a known maximum value of microamp current is fed to the input, e.g., with 10 microamps fed in, R3 is adjusted to give fulls cale reading on the meter, which now corresponds to 10 microamps. The milliammeter used should have a *linear* scale since this curve has a linear response.

The circuit can be made much simpler if a suitable NPN transistor is used (2N2712 or equivalent) since the collector current with zero signal is negligible and the meter will virtually read zero. Thus only one potentiometer is required, which is used for calibration. This simplified circuit is shown in Fig. 17-2.

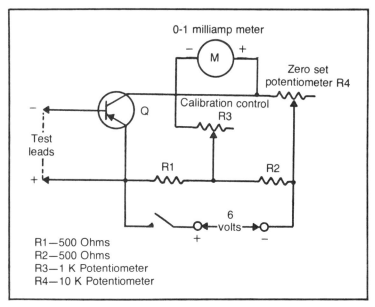

Fig. 17-1. Sensitive dc microammeter adjustable for full-scale reading of 10 microamps.

TRANSISTOR TESTER

This is a more elaborate transistor tester (Fig. 17-3) enabling the two leakage currents I_{co} and I^1_{co}, and α or common emitter amplification factor to be measured by switching the current to appropriate positions. It is designed specifically to use with low or moderate power PNP transistors only.

The circuit has two controls. Switch S1 is a three-pole, four-

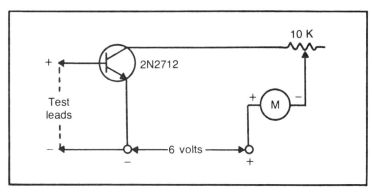

Fig. 17-2. Simple microammeter circuit using a NPN transistor type 2N2712, or equivalent. Meter again has a 0-1 milliamp movement.

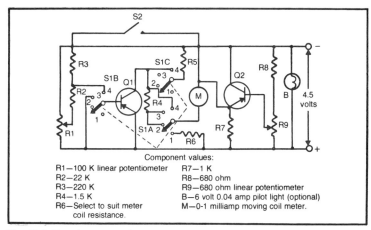

Fig. 17-3. Transistor tester for measuring leakage currents and common-emitter amplification factors (d) of PNP transistors.

way switch (SIA, SIB and SIC in the circuit) combined in one switch which is used for selecting the measurement to be taken. Potentiometer R9 is the reference control. Potentiometer R1 is the balance control. Switch S2 is a push button type used for the α measurement. An on-off switch is also needed in one battery lead. Transistor Q1 is HEP G0005. The transistor to be tested is plugged into the transistor socket connection at Q2 position. Other components are as specified in the figure.

The circuit is very easy to construct, but double-check all wiring connections in case the switch connections, in particular, have been wrongly made.

The tester is then used as follows:

1. Plug the transistor to be tested into the socket at Q2.

2. Switch on the circuit via the power switch.

3. Switch S1 to position 1 and adjust potentiometer R9 until the meter indicates exactly 2.5 volts.

4. Switch S1 to position 2. The meter reading will now indicate P'_{co} of Q2 in microamps. If the meter reading is zero, then the transistor is faulty (open circuit). If the meter reading is a maximum, then the transistor is faulty (short circuit).

5. Switch S1 to position 3. The meter reading will now indicate I_{co} of Q2 in microamps. Again if the meter reads zero or maximum, the transistor is faulty, as above.

6. Switch S1 to position 4 and adjust the balance (potentiometer R1) until the meter reads zero. If the transistor is faulty

133

(short circuit or open circuit) it will not be possible to adjust the meter to zero.

7. Press switch S2. The meter will now read the emitter base amplification factor (α) of Q2, full scale reading representing 100. If the meter reading is past full scale, then the α is greater than 100.

SIGNAL GENERATOR

This signal generator circuit (Fig. 17-4) oscillates at 80-1000 Hz and is designed for af signal injection for tracing faults in the audio end of receivers. It can also be used for signal injection at the rf end since the oscillations generated also contain strong af and i-f harmonics.

The construction should be kept as compact as possible, with short connections, as this will improve the stability of the oscillator. The ground line is extended by a wire terminating in an alligator clip to connect to the receiver ground. The output line is terminated in a short wire probe for tapping on to various parts in the receiver circuit.

CAPACITY TESTER

A Hartley oscillator can be used as a capacity meter for measuring the values of unknown capacitors. The complete circuit is shown in Fig. 17-5. The transformer used is a typical miniature transistor output transformer with a tapped primary. Capacitor C1 can be of fixed value (e.g., 0.1 μF) since the frequency of the oscillator is not important as long as it is in the audio range. C2 is then made the same value.

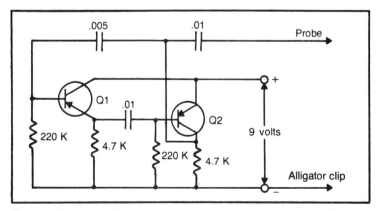

Fig. 17-4. Simple signal generator circuit with a frequency of about 1 kHz using HEP G0000, transistors for Q1 and Q2.

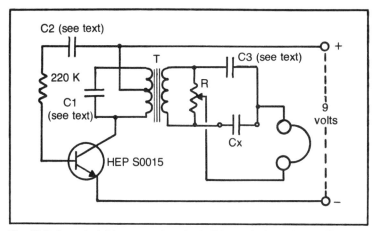

Fig. 17-5. Capacity bridge measuring circuit. T is a typical transistor radio output transformer. R is a 5 K linear potentiometer. Cx is capacitor of unknown value to be measured. Phones should be of high-impedance type.

The secondary of the transformer forms the test circuit which comprises an RC circuit consisting of a potentiometer R1, a capacitor of known value and close tolerance C3, and provision to connect capacitors of unknown value to complete a simple circuit. High impedance phones (or a high impedance earpiece) are connected across the center of the bridge.

To check the circuit, connect a capacitor of the *same* value as C3 in position Cx and set the potentiometer to its mid-position. No tone should be heard in the phones. Now adjust the potentiometer first one way and then the other. Movement away from mid-position should cause a tone to be heard, the strength of the tone rising with increasing adjustment from mid-position, either way. Check that the tone disappears at mid-position of the potentiometer and mark this position.

The setting of the potentiometer can now be calibrated to read capacitor ratios directly. Start by connecting a 1 μF capacitor in Cx position and find the adjustment point on the potentiometer where the bridge is balanced (i.e., the tone disappears). Mark this ×10. Now replace Cx with a 0.01 μF capacitor and find the balance point by turning the potentiometer the other way. Mark this ÷ 10.

Provided the potentiometer is a *linear* type, then the scale between ÷ 10 and 0 and 0 and × 10 can each be divided into ten equal divisions, enabling capacitor readings to be read off directly between 0.01 μF and 1 μF.

Note. For accurate calibration close tolerance capacitors must

135

be used. However, actual capacitance values are seldom critical, and so although realized capacity values of unknown capacitors may be as much as 100 percent out, this will have little significance in practice.

OHMMETER

Most electronic enthusiasts have a multimeter, which has facilities for resistance measurements. Lacking a multimeter, an ohmmeter can easily be made from a voltmeter, or milliammeter.

Figure 17-6 shows the circuit required to turn a voltmeter into an ohmmeter. Measurements is first made with the terminals A and B shorted, giving a meter reading of V1. The unknown resistance is then connected across A and B and the lower meter reading noted (V2).

The value of the unknown resistance can then be calculated as:

$$R_x = \frac{V_2 \times R_m}{V_1} - R_m$$

where R_m = resistance of meter (ohms)

By using a series of known resistors, it is possible to calibrate the meter scale to read ohms directly, i.e., starting from 0 (A and B shorted), and noting meter positions when, say 1 K, 2 K, 3 K, etc., resistors are connected across AB.

Because of the high resistance of a voltmeter, this circuit will not measure low resistance accurately (e.g., resistances between 200-300 ohms).

Figure 17-7 shows the circuit required to turn a milliammeter into an ohmmeter. The potentiometer R1 is adjusted to give full

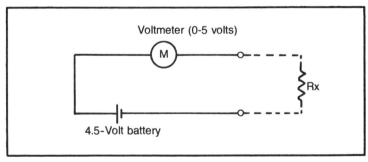

Fig. 17-6. Using a voltmeter as an ohmmeter. Scale can be calibrated to read ohms (see text). For a 0-10-volt meter, use a 9-volt battery.

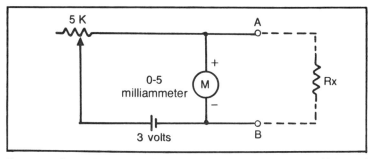

Fig. 17-7. Circuit for using a 0-5 milliammeter as an ohmmeter. Values of unknown resistance Rx are calculated (see text), or the meter scale re-calibrated to indicate ohms direct.

scale deflection on the meter with terminals A and B open. The unknown resistance is then connected across A and B and the meter reading noted. The value of this resistance can then be calculated as follows:

$$R_x = \frac{I \times R_m}{I_o - I}$$

where I = current reading with R_x connected
I_o = current with AB open (full scale)
R_m = resistance of milliammeter.

Again using a series of known resistances in turn for R_F the meter can be calibrated to read ohms directly (with full scale deflection = 0 ohms). This circuit is suitable for measuring low resistance values.

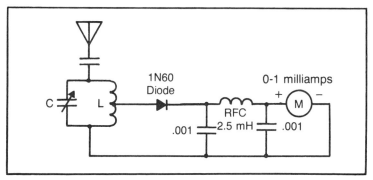

Fig. 17-8. Simple field strength meter using proprietary aerial coil L and matching tuning capacitor C.

137

FIELD-STRENGTH METER

This field-strength meter (Fig. 17-8) is basically an elementary receiver which will detect any transmission present to which the tuned circuit C and L is tuned, indicating the strength of the signal on the milliammeter. In the presence of relatively strong signals, no external aerial should be necessary. However, for weaker signal detection, an external aerial will be necessary. For a portable field strength meter, housed in a small box, this aerial can be of the telescopic type, preferably a submultiple of the resonant length of the transmitter frequency.

The only variable circuit components are L and C1 which are selected according to the transmitter band or frequency range required. For checking model radio control or CB transmitters, where the frequency covered is 27 MHz, the following specification for the coil (L) can be used:

Ten turns of 28 gauge enameled wire wound on a miniature (¼ inch) diameter coil former. Matching value of C1 is 20 pF. Final adjustment should be made against a transmitter known to be radiating, adjusting C1 until maximum signal strength is indicated on the meter. The field strength meter will then be broadly tuned to the 27 MHz band.

Rf SIGNAL GENERATOR

This very simple circuit (Fig. 17-9), using a silicon diode, is a useful rf signal generator for adjusting the front end of a superhet receiver circuit, particularly for FM working. R1 is a potentiometer enabling the dc current flowing through the diode to be adjusted, thus varying the amount of rf noise fed to the receiver via the probe.

Ideally, for VHF working, the probe should be connected by coaxial cable with the outer sheathing connected to the receiver ground. Note that only a silicon diode can be used in this circuit.

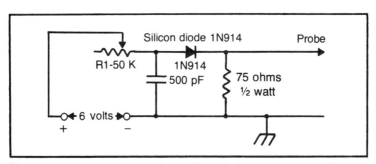

Fig. 17-9. Rf signal generator using a silicon diode type 1N21, or similar.

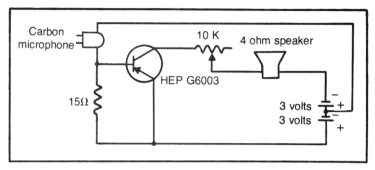

Fig. 17-10. A very simple baby alarm circuit. The potentiometer acts as a volume control.

INEXPENSIVE BABY ALARM

This very simple circuit (Fig. 17-10) is capable of giving excellent loudspeaker volume from a single transistor amplifier and sound input via a carbon microphone (not a crystal type). The microphone should be placed as near as possible to the noise source. It is then connected by two wires to the alarm circuit which can be built on a small panel. Speaker, panel and the battery can be fitted into a suitable enclosure or cabinet, together with a two-pole on-off switch.

Exactly the same circuit design can be used to make a loudspeaker or electronic megaphone. In this case a large cone should be fitted to the speaker to give directional characteristics to the sound output.

Another possible application of this circuit is for an indoor public address system!

CURRENT SAVERS

A transistor used as an amplifier in a relay input circuit (Fig. 17-11) will considerably improve the sensitivity of the relay, i.e., make it pull it at very much lower signal currents than in a straightforward circuit. Additional dc input is, of course, required to power the amplifier circuit. Current drain in this circuit can, however, be kept quite low.

The basic circuit shown is for a general purpose PNP transistor. The relay coil resistance represents the collector load, and the transistor type should be chosen accordingly. The current required to operate the relay is predetermined by the relay design and relay adjustment. The signal current required to operate the relay, however, is lower by approximately the current amplification factor of

139

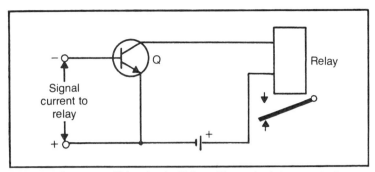

Fig. 17-11. Simple amplifying circuit which enables a relay to be operated by very much lower signal currents than usual.

the transistor in the common emitter configuration.

For conventional sensitive relay coil resistance of the order of 1000-2000 ohms, and operating currents of the order of 1 to 2 milliamps, general purpose switching transistors should provide work with input signal currents of the order of 10-20 microamps.

RAIN ALARM

This simple circuit (Fig. 17-2) detects moisture collecting on the sensor plate, triggering the transistor into condition and pulling in the relay. This closes the circuit to operate the alarm bell.

The sensor plate is made by sticking a piece of aluminum or copper foil onto a piece of perfboard. Zigzag cuts are then made

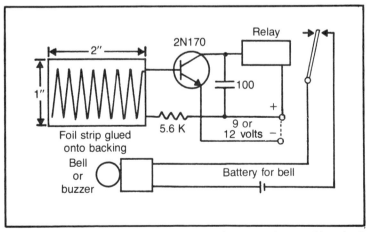

Fig. 17-12. Complete rain alarm with sensor plate and relay switching circuit operating a bell or buzzer. For the transistor type shown relay coil resistance should be 1000 ohms.

140

through the foil, using a stout modeling knife so that the two halves of the foil are physically separated by a narrow gap. The closer the gap, the more sensitive the plate will be to moisture collecting on it. Alternatively, the sensor plate can be etched from printed sheet stock.

The sensor is mounted outdoors, inclined at an angle of about 45 degrees. It is connected to the alarm circuit via two thin insulated wires. No adjustment is required other than to check that the alarm operates when the two halves of the foil are shorted out.

The transistor and alarm circuits can be powered by a single 9- or 12-volt battery. If the bell or buzzer proves to draw too much current, causing the relay to drop out, then a separate battery circuit can be used for the bell (taken through the relay contacts). Alternatively, a latching-type relay circuit can be used.

STABILIZED DC SUPPLY

This circuit (Fig. 17-13) provides a very stable dc output from a mains transformer output. Two outputs are provided, one of nominal 13 volts with a maximum current drain of 150 milliamps; and one giving a *stabilized* 11 volt 50 milliamp output. Stability of the latter is maintained within plus or minus 5 percent by the zener diode.

Note that this is a positive ground supply. Physical ground connection should be made between the positive line and the ground in the mains plug.

DISTRIBUTOR DWELL INDICATOR

This simple indicator (Fig. 17-4) can be used to measure the

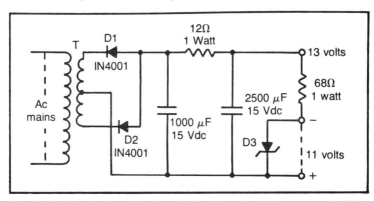

Fig. 17-13. This circuit provides two stabilized dc outputs from ac supply. T is a transformer with step-down ratio to give 12.6-volt output. Both resistors must have a rating of 1 watt or higher.

dwell or closure time of the points in a car distributor. The actual circuit comprises one diode, a resistor, a potentiometer, and one capacitor mounted on a suitable panel together with a milliammeter and 1.5-volt battery. Panel shape and size should be proportioned so that the complete instrument can easily be held in the hand. Leads are taken from the two points of the circuit shown, each terminating in an alligator clip.

To set up the indicator, short the two alligator clips and adjust the potentiometer until the meter reads a full scale deflection.

To use the indicator, clip the leads on to the ignition circuit so that they are effectively across the distributor points. With the engine running the meter should indicate a steady reading at some lower level. Since a zero meter reading represents points open and a full scale reading points closed, this steady position is a direct measure of the proportion of open to closed times, e.g., a steady reading of 1 (when the full scale reading is 5) would indicate 1/5th closed time or a dwell of $360/5 = 72$ degrees. The meter can, in fact, be calibrated in degrees dwell time for direct reading.

It can be noted that the circuit is not fed by the distributor, i.e., the meter is only influenced by its own battery. The diode blocks any voltage from the distributor circuit reaching the meter. The capacitor shorts to each peak voltage that occurs whenever the points open, and thus protects the diode and meter from such voltage peaks.

INVERTERS

Inverters are circuits which can step up (or step down) dc voltages, in the same way that a transformer can step up (or down) ac voltages. A transformer is still used in an inverter, but the

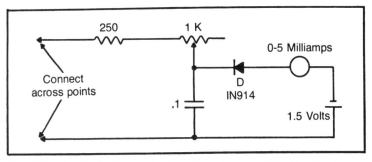

Fig. 17-14. Dwell indicator circuit using a diode for current "blocking," so that the meter simply reads "on" or "off," corresponding to closure or opening of points, respectively.

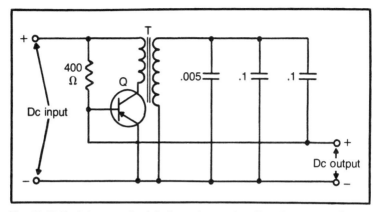

Fig. 17-15. Basic inverter circuit for low volt operation. Transformer ratio chosen for step-up required (see text).

primary circuit must also incorporate some means of transforming the dc input into ac for the transformer coupling to work. In the secondary circuit, rectification must be introduced to turn the ac induced in the secondary coil into dc again at the output. This dc-to-dc step-up is considerably more complicated than ac step-up (or step-down). If an inverter is to step-up a dc voltage to an ac voltage then, of course, rectification is not needed in the secondary circuit and the output can be tapped directly from the secondary. However, there may be a need for smoothing the output via capacitors.

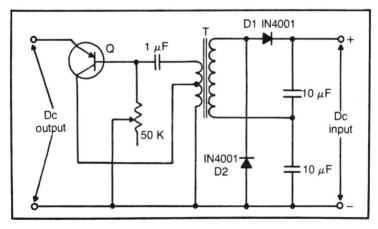

Fig. 17-16. Inverter circuit for higher power working. Q is an NPN type power transistor. Diodes D1 and D2 are silicon type. Transformer ratio selected according to the voltage step-up required.

143

The usual demand is to step-up a dc input voltage, rather than step it down. The principle of working the inverter is the same in both cases. It is simply a matter of using step-down or step-up ratio on the transformer, with the resistance of the primary matching the output requirements of the transistor ac generator, or oscillator.

A basic inverter circuit is shown in Fig. 17-15. This is suitable for low voltage operation, e.g., dc input voltage of up to 3 using an HEP G0005 or equivalent transistor. Voltage step-up ratio is approximately one-half of the transformer ratio, e.g., a 1:20 transformer ratio should give a dc output voltage of 15 volts from a 1.5 volt input. Efficiency, defined as *power out* (volts × current drain) divided by *power in* should be of the order of 75 percent.

An experimenter's circuit for higher working power is shown in Fig. 17-16, using a power transistor in the oscillator circuit. The oscillator is a Hartley type using a miniature transformer with a center tapped primary. The potentiometer forms a potential divider in the primary circuit which permits the output voltage to be adjusted over a fairly wide range.

Chapter 18

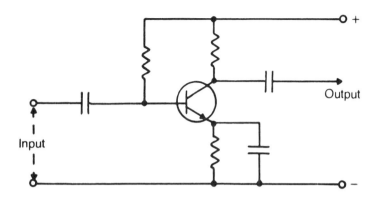

Integrated Circuits

The transistor certainly revolutionized electronics, but after some thirty-odd years it can now be regarded as old hat (but still the simplest, cheapest component for constructing simple circuits). It has been outdated—but certainly not made obsolete—by the *integrated circuit*, or IC, which has opened up a further new era in microelectronic technology.

How the IC developed is simple. After standardizing on production techniques for transistors, it became obvious that the same methods of photoetching could be used to produce complete circuits and subcircuits in a single package or "chip." At the same time the transistors and resistors incorporated in such circuits could be miniaturized to an extreme since they did not need individual cans or bodies to encapsulate them. Thus, complete circuits could be produced in physical sizes similar to those of transistors—and in fact many ICs have the same size and shape as transistors.

That was only the beginning. It was soon found that far more extreme miniaturization was possible. By adopting micro-techniques, a single chip could be produced containing as many as 50 separate components in a piece of silicon only 1/20th of an inch square. Also, from the manufacturing point of view, a larger piece of silicon known as a *wafer* could accommodate several hundred chips, so that a batch of wafers processed together could produce several thousand IC chips simultaneously. This is typical of small-scale integration or SSI.

From there medium-scale integration (MSI) was developed with a component density of more than 100 per chip; and large-scale integration (LSI) with a component density as high as 1000 components or more per chip. All use similar manufacturing techniques. It is simply a matter of scaling down and down in physical size.

There are however, some limitations with the manufacture of IC chips. Transistors and diodes are easy to form directly on the surface of the chip in the tiniest possible sizes. Resistors are not *quite* so easy. They can be produced in the form of micro-sized strips, or in the diffused areas, covering values from about 10 ohms to 30 kilohms with a tolerance of around plus or minus 10 percent. For higher values up to 50 kilohms and lower tolerances, resistors need to be produced by thin-film technique. For higher values still it is possible to "cheat" and use a transistor instead of a resistor, associated with a circuit which biases it to cut-off point.

Capacitors do present problems. To produce them in larger values they need to be relatively large in area, or quite out of scale with the rest of the chip components. Thus capacitors, except for small values, are commonly left out of IC circuits. To complete the circuit then requires a capacitor or capacitors in addition to the IC chip, connected externally. Thus *complete* working circuits using ICs are commonly made up from ICs together with additional discrete components.

This can still save a lot of time and effort in building a circuit. Also, especially in the case of more complex circuits, there is less chance of anything going wrong. All the major circuit components are inside the chip, correctly interconnected. It only remains to connect external components to the correct IC pins.

There can also be a considerable cost saving, too. The fact that IC chips can be produced thousands at a time means that the unit cost per chip is very low. So the IC can be sold at a relatively low price (not much more than that of a single transistor in some cases). Also it may contain dozens of components, and the cost of individual transistors and resistors to build the same circuit from separate (discrete) components could be considerably greater than that of the equivalent IC.

There is just one small snag remaining, though. Each IC is designed for a specific duty—a purpose-built circuit, in fact. Thus for a particular application you need a specific type of IC and enough information as to how it can be turned into a working circuit. It thus lacks flexibility for adapting to other types of circuit. You cannot

146

modify or change the IC circuit performance as you can with individual transistors.

Exceptions are *IC arrays* which comprise a number of *individual* components in the chip, not interconnected. These can be a very cheap source of diodes and transistors for experimental circuits. Even if you only use part of an IC array you may still show considerable savings over the purchase of individual diodes and transistors for many circuits.

IC PACKAGES

ICs come in many different package forms (Fig 18-1). Many of the simpler ones are similar in size and shape to transistors, only readily identified by the fact that they usually have more than three leads emerging from the base.

The more complex ICs are in the form of flat packages with leads emerging from each side, outwards or downwards. The three basic configurations are:

☐ *Dual-in-line*– the leads are on both sides and bent downwards at a right angle to form two separate and parallel rows. This package form is designed to allow the IC to be plugged directly into an integrated circuit holder or into a printed circuit panel, ready for soldering in place.

☐ *Quad-in-line*– like dual-in-line but with two parallel rows of leads on each side. Again for plugging into an IC holder or printed-circuit board.

☐ *Flat*– where the leads emerge horizontally outwards from each side.

The actual number of leads on a given IC can vary, but with a flat package, in invariably an even number with an equal number on each side, the total number involved is (usually) 12, 14, or 16, but may be as many as 24. Leads are identified by *pin numbers* starting with 1 at top left (looking down at the top of the IC), down that (left) side and then back up the other side ending at top right. To "read" looking at the bottom of the IC, start at top right.

Pin numbers are not marked on the IC—there is no room for that—but they are the only clue for connections required. If you have a specification sheet for the IC, the complete allocation of pin numbers will be given. If you are working from a circuit drawing incorporating an IC, pin numbers will be shown alongside the IC in

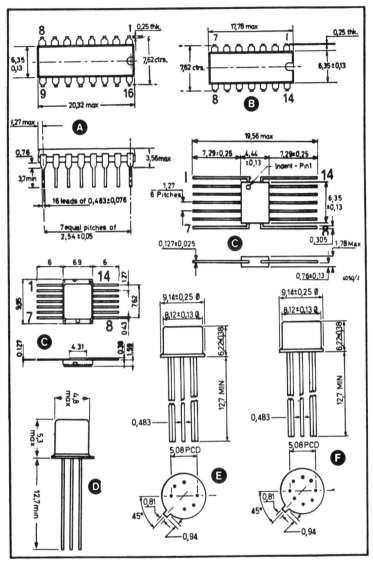

Fig. 18-1. Examples of IC packages—larger than actual size.

"convenient" order. This is often quite different from the actual position (or true numbering) of the pins on the IC itself, which is a point to be watched. Without *any* indication of pin numbers on the circuit drawing you will be lost. So, before you start building an IC circuit from a drawing, make sure the pin numbers are there. It will be hopeless trying to use guesswork.

148

Apart from that, treat an IC as you would any other component when building a circuit, but making sure you do identify and connect up all the pin numbers correctly. Note here that in many circuits designed around ICs not all the pin numbers are used. Do not try connecting them to ground or anywhere else unless you know what the IC circuit is. Unallocated pin numbers represent entry to components or subcircuits inside the IC which are *not* required or used in that particular circuit design.

IC RECEIVER PROJECTS

Integrated circuit LM372 is a "complete" radio receiver circuit. Complete, that is, except that it needs to be matched to a tuned circuit and a "listening device"—plus one capacitor to complete the internal circuitry of the IC. That makes a very simple circuit to build—(Fig. 18-2).

The tuned circuit is a standard miniature ferrite rod inductor and tuning capacitor (0-500 pF) connected to the "input" of the IC (pin 2) via a .01 μF capacitor to "match" the tuned circuit to the IC. The .01 μF capacitor between pins 1 and 3, and connecting pin 4 to

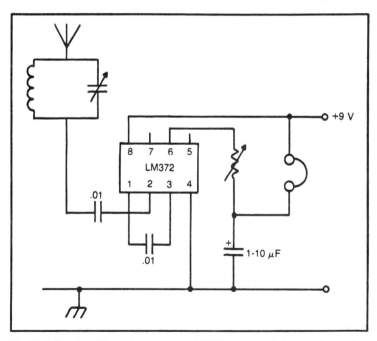

Fig. 18-2. Simple radio receiver based on LM372 integrated circuit and powering headphones.

149

ground completes the IC circuit. Output is then taken from pin 6 to "phones" via a 5 kilohm potentiometer. Start with this set at *maximum* resistance and turn down until a reasonable signal is received in the phones. A capacitor from one side of the phones to ground can help performance. Try values from 1 to 10 μF. Note in this diagram the IC pins have been allocated in true sequential order.

The performace of this circuit will be fairly poor. If you get no performance at all, try connecting pin 7 to ground via a 1 μF capacitor; also pin 5 to ground with a .01 μF capacitor. Performance should be better, but probably still not very powerful. Adding a single stage of transistor amplification will improve it to the extent where it will work a small (2-inch) 8-ohm loudspeaker quite well (Fig. 18-3). The transformer required is a midget audio transformer with a turn ratio of around 100:1. (If the transformer you buy has a center tap, ignore this tap and connect across the primary ends of the transformer.) If you want a volume control, insert a 1 kilohm potentiometer in the base lead of the transistor.

How about adding another stage of amplification? Well, this time let's try using another IC— the LM386. The added-on circuit is then as shown in Fig. 18-4. Note that the IC has been drawn with a

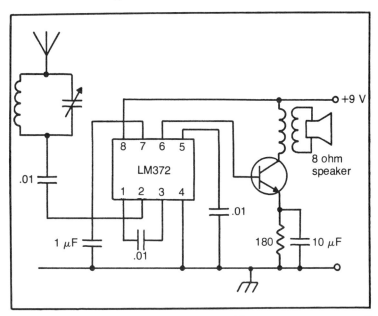

Fig. 18-3. Improved circuit with transistor amplifier stage to power a small loudspeaker. Transistor is 2N2219, or equivalent.

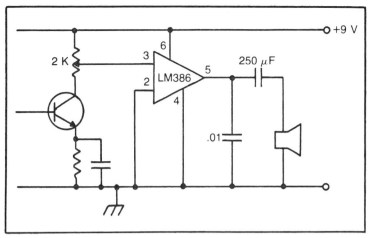

Fig. 18-4. Extended circuit with additional stage of amplification provided by a second IC.

triangular symbol this time (which is the usual way of showing an IC amplifier). Also the pin numbers are designated in random fashion this time.

For the collector load of the transistor use a 2-kilohm potentiometer, which will both enable you to adjust the input to the IC to match and prevent swamping, and act as a volume control (with more resistance turned in).

Now you should have quite a nice and extremely simple working receiver, but one that is still capable of further improvement using parts of the IC circuit still untapped. (Pins 1, 7, and 8 have not been used.) Try connecting them with further discrete components as shown in Fig. 18-5. You can always go back to the previous circuit if this does not work as well.

SIMPLE IC LOGIC PROJECT

Logic gates, flip-flops, memories, counters, etc., are all readily available in IC packages—the list available is almost endless and growing all the time. They are used as building blocks to produce sophisticated circuits right up to microprocessors and computers.

Probably the simplest of these devices to start with for building working circuits are logic circuits that "count"—commonly based on monostable vibrators, which convert circuit input pulses into output current pulses of constant current and duration.

The SAK 140 is such a device which, with a minimum of added components can readily be used to make a revolution counter for

151

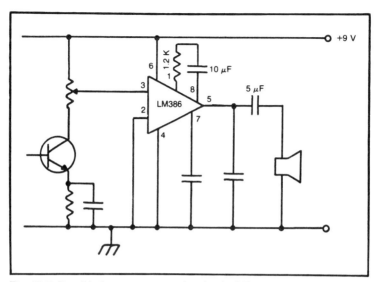

Fig. 18-5. Possible improvements to the circuit of Fig. 18-4.

autos, boat engines, etc., using contact breaker ignition. The circuit shown in Fig. 18-6 is specific to this particular IC, but there are many others like it which can be used in the same way—provided the correct pin numbers to use can be identified.

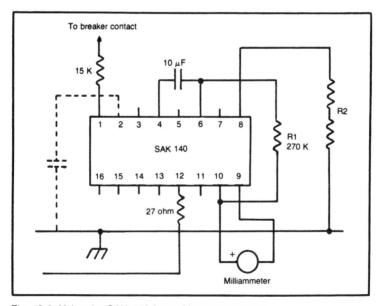

Fig. 18-6. Using the SAK 140 for making a rev counter.

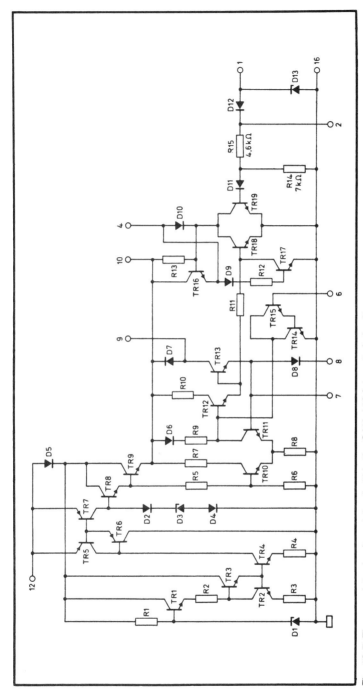

Fig. 18-7. The complete circuit contained within the SAK 140 integrated circuit.

153

With the SAK 140 you do, in fact, get quite a lot of circuitry for your money in a single 16-pin flat package. The complete circuit contained in the chip is shown in Fig. 18-7. Imagine building that from discrete components.

The complete working circuit of Fig. 18-6 shows that only 8 pins need actually be used. Pin 1 connects to the contact breaker whose value is chosen to ensure that input current does not exceed 10 mA (a 15 kilohm resistor is correct for a 12 V ignition circuit); but the IC itself also incorporates internal protection via diodes. The supply (positive) can be 10-18 volts (standard 12 V auto battery voltage is ideal), connecting (positive) to pin 12 via a low value resistor. (Again internal circuitry in the IC protects it against reversal of supply voltage polarity.) Pins 4 and 6 are connected with a 10 μF capacitor (metallized-polyester type preferred); and pins 6 and 8 with a 270 kilohm resistor. A 0-50 milliammeter connects between pins 9 and 10, leaving a variable resistor to be connected to pin 8 and ground to work as an adjustment for peak current output. Note also that pin 16 is connected to ground.

Ideally resistor R2 should comprise one fixed resistor and one variable resistor with a total series resistance of 120-270 ohms, e.g., try 20 ohms for the fixed resistor and 100 or 200 ohms for a variable resistor. If the meter reading is hesitant or flickering instead of steady, try adjusting the value of R1 up and down. This may be necessary to get steady readings at low engine rpm. Meter reading is linear and can be calibrated at one point against a known engine speed.

Chapter 19

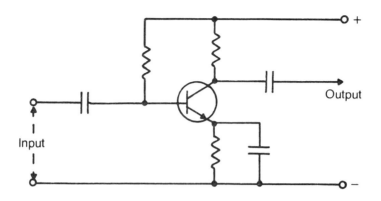

Additional Projects

If you want to switch high power by a solid-state device then a triac is the obvious choice. Figure 19-1 shows the basic circuit for a triac power switch. Closing the manually operated switch turns the triac "on" in the load circuit.

POWER SWITCHES

The obvious question at this point is why use a triac at all if you have to use an ordinary switch to turn it on? The answer is that a suitable triac can pass quite high currents which could burn an ordinary switch (or call for a heavy duty switch to avoid this). In this circuit the mechanical switch (S) has only to carry a momentary high circuit when first closed. After that, when the triac has switched on, the current through the mechanical switch drops to a negligible value.

The resistors R1 and R2 are used as current limiting devices in the mechanical switch and triac drive circuits, respectively. The value of R1 is chosen to limit the first surge of current to an acceptable figure, but must not be too high, otherwise it will tend to delay the turn-on of the triac itself.

Resistor R2 is used to limit the current flowing through the triac in its turned-on condition, according to the specified performance of the device. In the case of the IRT82, maximum current rating is 8 amps at 120 V. From Ohm's law it follows that the

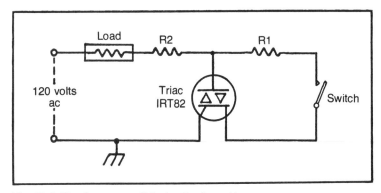

Fig. 19-1. Simple power switch circuit using a triac.

minimum total resistance in the triac drive circuit (load plus R2) must be 120 ÷ 8 = 15 ohms.

This has to be considered along with the load rating, i.e., the maximum current which can be allowed to flow through the load itself. The *lower* of these two values will determine the value of R2 required.

For example, suppose the load rating is 120 watts. Since current = watts ÷ volts, the *maximum* current that can be obtained to flow through the triac drive current is 120 ÷ 120 = 1 amp. Using Ohm's law again:

$$\text{resistance} = \frac{\text{volts}}{\text{amps}}$$

$$= \frac{120}{1}$$

$$= 120 \text{ ohms}$$

Thus the combined value of load resistance and R2 must be 120 ohms. If in doubt, or the load resistance is known to be quite low, ignore it and use the value calculated above for R1.

Improved Circuit

Figure 19-2 shows an improved triac switch circuit incorporating a 0.1 μF capacitor as an additional component. The triggering current is now governed by C rather than R1, so a higher value may be used for R1 to limit the peak turn-on current flowing through switch S. In this case R1 can be made 100 ohms or even 200

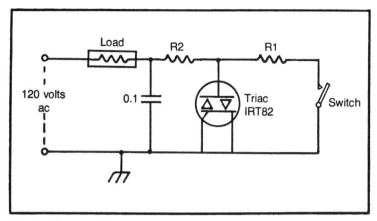

Fig. 19-2. Improved triac power switch circuit.

ohms. The value of R2 is again chosen to limit the current flowing through the triac when switched on. Note: This circuit must be used when the load is inductive (e.g., a vibrator or electric motor). The first circuit will only work properly with a noninductive load (e.g., a lamp).

Dc Triggered Triac Switch

Figure 19-3 shows a dc triggered triac power switch, i.e., the power circuit is switched on via a low voltage dc supply and switch. The capacitor is only necessary if the load is inductive.

Replacing the Mechanical Switch

In any of these three circuits the mechanical switch (S) shown

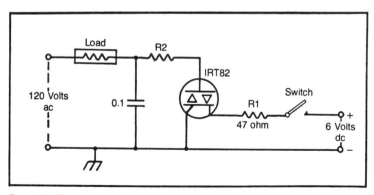

Fig. 19-3. Triac power switch triggered by a dc signal.

157

can be replaced by a transistor switch circuit, thus providing an all solid state circuit. The main requirement is to limit the initial surge circuit through the transistor switch circuit to a suitable level by using a high enough value for R1. *Construction note:* Since the triac in the power circuit can be carrying high currents (up to 8 amps with the type shown), the triac itself must be mounted in a suitable heat-sink.

ELECTRONIC BURGLAR ALARM

Figure 19-4 shows a very simple electronic alarm circuit using a small SCR working off a low voltage battery. The alarm can be a bell or buzzer drawing a reasonably small current, say not much more than 1 amp, when the battery required should have a voltage about 1 V more than the normal operating voltage of the bell or buzzer.

Besides being easy to construct this circuit has several other attractive features. It can be left connected for long periods before battery replacement is required because, in the standing ready state, the current drain is only a few milliamps. A test switch can be incorporated where shown to check that the alarm is working properly (i.e., operating the test switch should operate the alarm).

Virtually any number of type of activating switches can be wired into the circuit via leads running to any required length. It is merely a matter of choosing the right type of switch for the purpose—e.g., a "press-to-open" switch that closes (i.e., switches

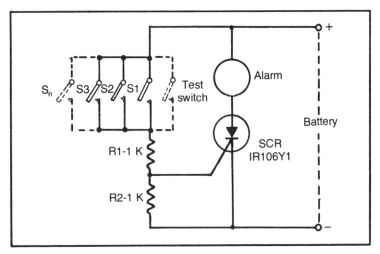

Fig. 19-4. Basic electronic burglar alarm circuit using an SCR.

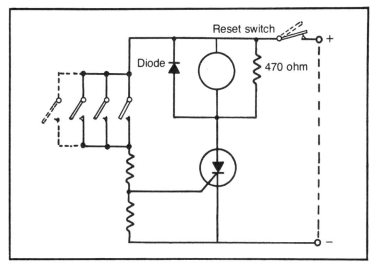

Fig. 19-5. Burglar alarm circuit with latching facility.

on) when a window is opened; or a "press-to-close" switch under a pressure pad or mat that switches "on" when pressure is applied.

LATCHING BURGLAR ALARM CIRCUIT

The simple alarm circuit can be improved by the addition of one extra resistor, R3, wired across the alarm in series with a normally-on switch, as shown in Fig. 19-5. This resistor acts as a latch, holding the alarm circuit closed after it is activated by first closure of any of switches S1, S2, S3, etc. In other words, a continual alarm signal does not depend on the initiating switch remaining operated. The reset switch is necessary to break the alarm circuit once triggered and restore it to the standing ready state.

"FOOLPROOF" BURGLAR ALARM

The disadvantage of the first two burglar alarm circuits is that if either of the leads running to the first switch (S1) are cut the whole circuit is rendered inoperative. Equally any switch, once its position has been detected, is rendered inoperative by cutting one of its leads.

This limitation can be overcome by connecting the switches S1, S2, S3, etc., in series, as shown in Fig. 19-6. In this case the latching resistor R2 is essential. Now, if any of the switches S1, S2, S3, etc., are operated (opened) *or* the wires are cut the circuit

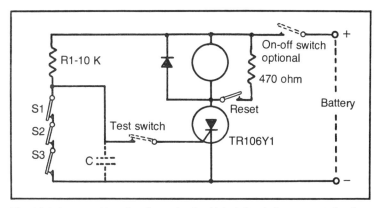

Fig. 19-6. Improved burglar alarm circuit which defies being put out of action.

latches on to keep the alarm sounding. (Note the types of switches used have to work the opposite way around to the power circuits—break for "on".)

There are two disadvantages to this circuit. One is that vibration or an accidental knock could open a switch and set off a false alarm. This can be overcome by connecting a 1 μF capacitor (C) across the switches as shown dotted in the diagram. The other disadvantage is that it draws a higher standby current in the non-operated state. This can be minimized by using a high value for R1, but if the rate of R1 is increased too much there will come a point when the SCR will not switch on. So you really have to accept a shorter battery life and a test switch should be incorporated to check the battery condition from time to time. This must also be of the normally-closed type.

THERMOSTAT-CONTROLLED HEATERS

The high current capacity of triacs can be used to advantage in heater controls, using a simple thermostat with a low circuit rating as a master device to switch on at a pre-set temperature. The circuit (Fig. 19-7) is virtually the same as that of a basic power switch, with resistor R1 limiting the initial surge current through the thermostat contacts.

This particular circuit provides two modes of operation—manual, (direct switching on by by-passing the thermostat) and automatic together with an intermediate "off" position.

The number of heaters which can be switched by the triac is dependent on the maximum power rating of the triac used. For an IRTS2 this is only 960 watts (on 120 volts supply), which would be

160

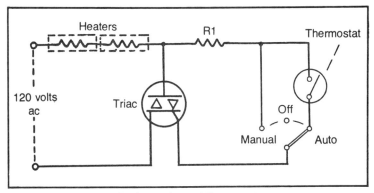

Fig. 19-7. Heater control using a triac and thermostat.

sufficient for powering small heaters, but not electric furnaces. Select a triac matched to the power actually required.

SIMPLE FIELD-STRENGTH METERS

Four components only are required for making a simple field strength meter—a coil (L), diode (D), capacitor (C), and a small microammeter (Fig. 19-8). The antenna can be a "whip" of thin wire, or just a length of insulated wire (e.g., for looping around the antenna of a transmitter you want to test and is known to have a very weak signal).

The turning of such a circuit is fairly broad but nominally specified by the values of the coil and capacitor. In other words the turned circuit will resonate, or show maximum meter reading when the frequency received is equal to:

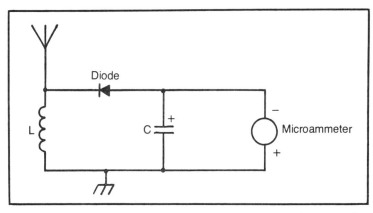

Fig. 19-8. Simple field-strength meter using minimum number of components.

$$\frac{1}{6.28 \sqrt{L \times C}} \times 10^6$$

where L = coil inductance in microhenries (μH)

C = capacitance value in picofarads (pF)

It is easiest to work this formula as a *product* of the inductance and capacitance required, i.e.,

$$L \times C = \frac{0.025}{f^2} \times 10^{12}$$

where f is the required resonant frequency

Thus if you want the resonant frequency to be, say 500 kHz:

$$LC = \frac{0.025}{(500)^2} \times 10^{12}$$

$$= 0.001 \times 10^8 \text{ (approx)}$$

Thus if you used .001 μF capacitor (= 1000 pF)

Required value of $L = \dfrac{0.025 \times 10^{12}}{500^2 \times 1000}$

$$= 100 \text{ microhenries}$$

$$= 0.1 \ \mu\text{H}$$

Work out values required in this way, starting with a guess-imated value for C. In practice remember the actual value of C with an electrolytic capacitor may be very much different from its normal value—as much as 20% down or 50% or even 100% up. You can then improve the circuit by making it tunable, e.g., using a variable

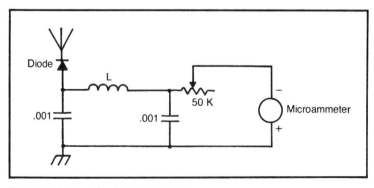

Fig. 19-9. Tunable field-strength meter.

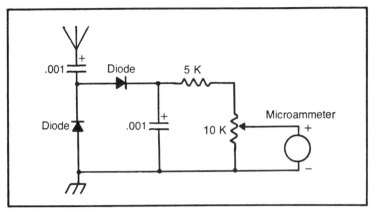

Fig. 19-10. Field-strength meter adjustable over a wide range of frequencies.

capacitor for C covering the range of capacitors required to resonate over a given frequency range. For a simple solution, try using a variable resistor in a slightly modified circuit (Fig. 19-9).

The final circuit (Fig. 19-10) shows a fixed straight meter that is not frequency selective and can be used to detect a wide range of frequencies, adjusting sensitivity by means of the 10 K pot.

HIGH-IMPEDANCE VOLTMETER

This simple circuit (Fig. 19-11) makes a highly sensitive dc voltmeter capable of measuring in three ranges—0-1 V, 0-10 V and

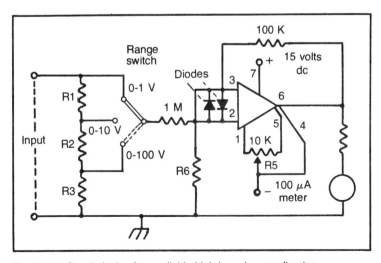

Fig. 19-11. Circuit design for a reliable high-impedance voltmeter.

163

0-100 V. Its accuracy depends on the tolerance of the resistors used—R1, R2, R3, and R4. Choose fine tolerance resistors identified by a red (2 percent tolerance) or preferably brown (1 percent tolerance) band following the color code band. Metal-oxide type resistors are preferred.

Resistor R5 is a 100 K pot (perferably one with linear characteristics) and its purpose is to provide adjustment for setting the meter to zero. The diodes are general-purpose silicon type, R6 being a suitable value of load resistor calculated as:

$$R6 = \frac{15}{I_{max}}$$

where I_{max} is the maximum rated forward current for the diodes used. (Use the next preferred value up from the calculated value of resistance.)

Heart of the circuit is a general FET op amp (LH0042C), connecting all seven pins as shown. The 15-volt supply is connected to pin 7 (positive) and pin 4 (negative). A rotary is used to switch the meter into the voltage range required.

IC RADIOS

The ZN414 integrated circuit is a complete basic TRF radio receiver circuit providing high gain. It is capable of working a low

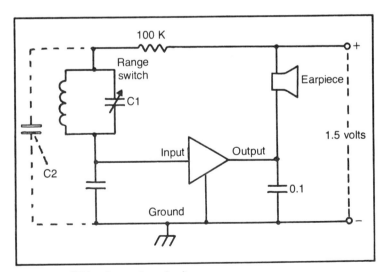

Fig. 19-12. TRF radio-receiver circuit.

164

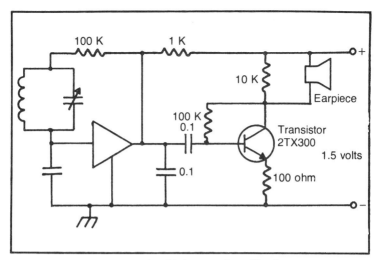

Fig. 19-13. Radio receiver with added stage of amplification.

impedance crystal earpiece when connected to a simple tuned circuit, the only other components needed being a couple of capacitors and 100 K resistor (Fig. 19-2). Battery supply is 1.4 V to 2.0 V. Any higher voltage will tend to produce unstable operation.

Coil L is 80 turns of 30 gauge wire close wound on a 1½" by ¼" diameter ferrite rod. The tuning capacitor C1 can be a 250 pF compression trimmer type. If the circuit does not appear to work properly, switch the connection of C2 to the opposite end of the tuned circuit (as shown dotted). Alternatively, if the output is too weak add a stage of transistor amplification as shown in Fig. 19-13.

Component numbers for the amplifier stage are for a 2TX300 (or equivalent) transistor. Peak output power should then be of the order of 500-600 mW, which should be enough to operate a minia-ture speaker; or if not, a high-impedance crystal earpiece.

For even more power output, i.e., to operate a speaker at good volume, additional stages of transistor amplification can be added, but this is a poor approach. The same result can be produced with far less components using an IC audio amplifier, as in Fig. 19-14.

The transistor used can be any general purpose af type (adjust values of R1 and R2 to suit if necessary). The IC is an MFC 4000B or MC3360P ¼-watt audio amplifier using all four pins. Increase the value of the resistor in the top line to 1M to accommodate the higher voltage required to drive the amplifier. The speaker used should have a nominal impedance of 16 ohms with a rated power of 390-500 mW.

165

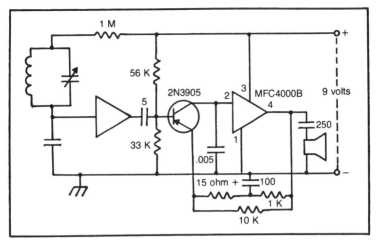

Fig. 19-14. Radio receiver using an IC audio amplifier.

LAMP DIMMER CIRCUIT

Theoretically at least a variable resistor (potentiometer) can work as a lamp dimmer on a main circuit, but there are several practical disadvantages. For a start the resistor would need to have a high power rating, and its construction capable of withstanding considerable heating. Also variable resistance is far from being the best method of variable control on ac circuits. A much more practical form of circuit is to use a triac as a power switch, phase-triggered by a diac, with a potentiometer as the overall variable power control.

The basic components then needed are a diac and triac together with the variable resistor (R1) and capacitor C1. R1 and C1 together provide a combined potential divider and variable phase shift. Resistor R2 may then be added as a limiting device to protect R1 against excessive current when set to minimum resistance, but is not strictly necessary (Fig. 19-15).

The only real disadvantage of this, as a simple circuit, is that it can generate electrical noise in the supply line which could affect other electronic items connected to the same line. This can be prevented by introducing a capacitor C2 and inductance (L1) as filter components, as shown dotted.

LONG-TIME-DELAY CIRCUIT

The simple circuit shown in Fig. 19-16 is a dc operated turn-on switch, which can be given a delay time between closing of switch S

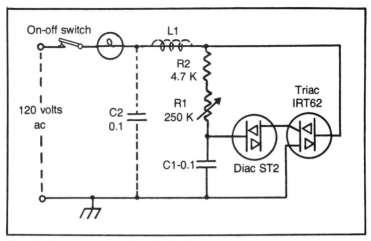

Fig. 19-15. Lamp dimmer circuit using triacs.

and the SCR actually switching on current through the load of up to nearly 10 minutes or more.

There is nothing critical about this circuit and the resistor values shown will match a 2N3702 transistor or equivalent. The value of C1 should be 0.1-0.01 μF and any general purpose silicon diode can be used.

The time delay realized is dependent on the values of C1 and R1 used, the higher these two values the longer the time delay. The

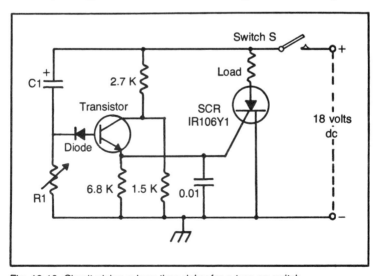

Fig. 19-16. Circuit giving a long time delay for a turn-on switch.

circuit should work with values for C1 from 1 μf to 1000 μF, and with values of R1 from 10 K to 500 K. Basically the higher the values of both C1 and R1 the longer the time delay.

It is possible to calculate the time delay for any combination of C1 and R1 but in practice the actual delay achieved will probably be quite different. This is mainly because capacitance values for large electrolytic capacitors are nominal rather than actual.

By using the highest value for C1—i.e., 1000 μF—and using a 500 K variable resistor of R1 it should be possible to achieve delays ranging from about 100 seconds up to 10 minutes. Toward the upper end of the pot movement (i.e., approaching its maximum resistance value), the circuit may not work. If this is so, substitute the next pot value down.

A safeguard with this circuit is to connect a 6.8 K or 10 K resistor in series with R1 in case the residual resistance of the pot in its minimum position is too low, allowing excess current to flow through the transistor and overload it.

WATER LEVEL ALARM

Try this circuit for a simple bilge-water level alarm for boats. Use short lengths of stainless steel or monel wire for the probes, mounted on a water resistant and insulated panel about 1 inch apart. Position in the boat so that the tips of the wire are at the level in the bilges at which you want the alarm to sound.

The circuit (Fig. 19-17) should be built on a separate panel

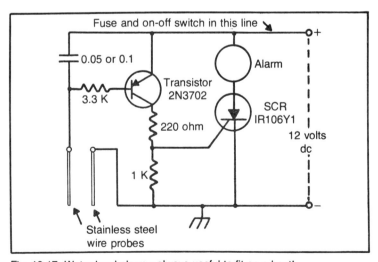

Fig. 19-17. Water level alarm—always useful to fit on a boat!

mounted well above the bilges in a dry place and connected by wires to the probes. Supply for this circuit can be taken from the boat's battery via a fuse and on-off switch. The former protects the battery in the event of circuit failure or accidental starting. The on-off switch disconnects the circuit when not required.

The circuit employs an SCR as a power switch, operating a buzzer or bell, that should have a nominal operating voltage of 8-10 V. The circuit remains open until the bilge water level reaches the probes when a moderately conductive path is established between the probes. The transistor ensures adequate amplification of the resulting current flow to trigger the SCR into its switching mode. Component values shown should suit a 2N3702 transistor or near equivalent.

Appendix

Common Abbreviations

Not all these abbreviations are to be found in this book, but this list can be useful when studying catalogues of components, etc., and for further reading.

A or amp	Ampere
AC	Alternating Current
AF	Audio Frequency
AFC	Automatic Frequency Control
AGC	Automatic Gain Control
AM	Amplitude Modulation
AVC	Automatic Volume Control
BA	British Association Screw Thread
BC	Bayonet Cap
BFO	Beat Frequency Oscillator
C	Capacitor
CW	Carrier Wave
D	Diode
DC	Direct Current
DCC	Double Cotton Covered
DPDT	Double Pole Double Throw
DPST	Double Pole Single Throw
DSC	Double Silk Covered
EMF	Electromotive Force (Voltage)
F	Farad

FET	Field Effect Transistor
FM	Frequency Modulation
FSD	Full Scale Deflection
H	Henry
Hertz or Hz	Cycles per Second
Hz	High Impedance
HF	High Frequency
HT	High Tension
I	Current
IC	Integrated Circuit
IF	Intermediate Frequency
IFT	Intermediate Frequency Transformer
k or kilo	1000
kHz	Kilohertz
kV	Kilovolts (100 volts)
L	Inductance
LF	Low Frequency
LZ	Low Impedance
M	Mega ($\times$ 1 million)
m	Milli ($\div$ 1000)
μ	Micro ($\div$ 1,000,000)
μA	Microamp
mA	Milliamp
μF	Microfarad
μH	Microhenry
mH	Millihenry
MCW	Modulated Carrier Wave
MHz	Megacycles (millions of cycles) per Second
mV	Millivolt
N	Nano ($\div$ 1,000,000,000)
Ω	Ohms
P	Primary
PU	Pick Up
pF	Picofarad
Q	Q Factor (of coil)
R	Resistor
RC	Resistance-Capacitance
RF	Radio Frequency
RFC	Radio Frequency Choke
RMS	Root Mean Squared
SBC	Small Bayonet Cap

SCC	Single Cotton Covered
SCR	Silicon Controlled Rectifier
SPDT	Single Pole Double Throw
SPST	Single Pole Single Throw
SSC	Single Silk Covered
S.W.G. or s.w.g.	Standard Wire Gauge
T	Transformer
TO	Transistor Outline
TR	Transistor
TRF	Tuned Radio Frequency
UHF	Ultra High Frequency (above 200 kHz)
V	Volt
VFO	Variable Frequency Oscillator
VHF	Very High Frequency (up to 200 kHz)
W	Watt
WT	Wireless Telegraphy, or Morse
X	Reactance
Z	Impedance
ZD	Zener Diode

Index

Other Bestsellers From TAB